How To Use This Study Guide

This 15-lesson study guide corresponds to *"The Miracles of Jesus"* (Renner TV). Each lesson in this study guide covers a topic that is addressed during the program series, with questions and references supplied to draw you deeper into your own private study of the Scriptures on this subject.

To derive the most benefit from this study guide, consider the following:

First, watch or listen to the program prior to working through the corresponding lesson in this guide. (Programs can also be viewed at **renner.org** by clicking on the Media/Archives links or on our Renner Ministries YouTube channel.)

Second, take the time to look up the scriptures included in each lesson. Prayerfully consider their application to your own life.

Third, use a journal or notebook to make note of your answers to each lesson's Study Questions and Practical Application challenges.

Fourth, invest specific time in prayer and in the Word of God to consult with the Holy Spirit. Write down the scriptures or insights He reveals to you.

Finally, take action! Whatever the Lord tells you to do according to His Word, do it.

For added insights on this subject, it is recommended that you obtain Rick Renner's book *Why We Need the Gifts of the Holy Spirit*. You may also select from Rick's other available resources by placing your order at **renner.org** or by calling 1-800-742-5593.

TOPIC

Capernaum, the City of Jesus

SCRIPTURES

1. **Luke 4:14-21** — And Jesus returned in the power of the Spirit into Galilee: and there went out a fame of him through all the region round about. And he taught in their synagogues, being glorified of all. And he came to Nazareth, where he had been brought up: and, as his custom was, he went into the synagogue on the sabbath day, and stood up for to read. And there was delivered unto him the book of the prophet Esaias. And when he had opened the book, he found the place where it was written, The Spirit of the Lord is upon me, because he hath anointed me to preach the gospel to the poor; he hath sent me to heal the brokenhearted, to preach deliverance to the captives, and recovering of sight to the blind, to set at liberty them that are bruised, to preach the acceptable year of the Lord. And he closed the book, and he gave it again to the minister, and sat down. And the eyes of all them that were in the synagogue were fastened on him. And he began to say unto them, This day is this scripture fulfilled in your ears.

2. **Luke 4:24, 28-31** — And he said, Verily I say unto you, No prophet is accepted in his own country. . . . And all they in the synagogue, when they heard these things, were filled with wrath, and rose up, and thrust him out of the city, and led him unto the brow of the hill whereon their city was built, that they might cast him down headlong. But he passing through the midst of them went his way, and came down to Capernaum, a city of Galilee, and taught them on the sabbath days.

SYNOPSIS

The 15 lessons in this study on *The Miracles of Jesus Christ* will focus on the following topics:

- Capernaum, the City of Jesus
- Jesus Casts an Unclean Spirit Out of a Notable Man
- Jesus Heals Peter's Mother-in-Law

A Note From Rick Renner

I am on a personal quest to see a "revival of the Bible" so people can establish their lives on a firm foundation that will stand strong and endure the test as the end-time storm winds begin to intensify.

In order to experience a revival of the Bible in your personal life, it is important to take time each day to read, receive, and apply its truths to your life. James tells us that if we will continue in the perfect law of liberty — refusing to be forgetful hearers but determined to be doers — we will be blessed in our ways. As you watch or listen to the programs in this series and work through this corresponding study guide, I trust that you will search the Scriptures and allow the Holy Spirit to help you hear something new from God's Word that applies specifically to your life. I encourage you to be a doer of the Word that He reveals to you. Whatever the cost, I assure you — it will be worth it.

> Thy words were found, and I did eat them;
> and thy word was unto me the joy and rejoicing of mine heart:
> for I am called by thy name, O Lord God of hosts.
> — Jeremiah 15:16

Your brother and friend in Jesus Christ,

Rick Renner

The Miracles of Jesus Christ

Copyright © 2019 by Rick Renner
1814 W. Tacoma St.
Broken Arrow, OK 74012-1406

Published by Rick Renner Ministries
www.renner.org

ISBN 13: 978-1-6803-1625-4

ISBN 13 eBook: 978-1-6803-1663-6

- Jesus Heals a Nobleman's Son
- Jesus Causes a Miraculous Catch of Fish
- Jesus Multiplies the Loaves and Fishes in Galilee
- Jesus Heals a Centurion's Servant
- Jesus Heals a Paralyzed Man Who Came Through the Roof
- Jesus Calms a Storm on the Sea of Galilee
- Jesus Casts a Legion of Demons Out of a Demoniac
- Jesus Heals a Woman With an Issue of Blood
- Jesus Raises Jairus' Daughter From Death to Life
- Jesus Heals a Man at the Pool of Bethesda
- Jesus Raises Lazarus From the Dead
- Jesus Restores Malchus' Ear and Raises a Boy From the Dead

The emphasis of this lesson:

Nazareth was Jesus' hometown, but after being rejected in it, He established His base of ministry in the prosperous and accommodating city of Capernaum. More miracles were done in Capernaum than in any other city in Israel.

Nazareth Was Jesus' Hometown

We know from Scripture that Jesus grew up in Nazareth (*see* Matthew 2:23). Luke 4:14-16 says that after He was baptized by John in the Jordan River and was tempted by the devil for 40 days in the wilderness, "Jesus returned in the power of the Spirit into Galilee: and there went out a fame of him through all the region round about. And he taught in their synagogues, being glorified of all. And he came to Nazareth, where he had been brought up...."

Nazareth was a very small, isolated town in lower Galilee. It had a tiny population, no major roads, and virtually no employment. The people of Nazareth were quite religious, had a small-world view, and were very close-minded to new ideas and newcomers. Basically, Nazareth was a "commuter" community to the luxurious city of Sepphoris, which was located about four miles to the north. It seems that Sepphoris was where Jesus' grandparents lived and where most of the people of Nazareth worked, including Joseph, Jesus' father, who was in the construction business.

Being a small, closed community, Nazareth was a place where everyone seemed to know each other. Such was the case with Jesus. The townspeople knew His father, His mother, His sisters, and His brothers (*see* Matthew 13:55, 56). Their familiarity with Jesus and His family caused the people to see Him as common and ordinary. Thus, they could not see Him for who He really was, and consequently, could not receive Him as the Messiah sent by God. Nazareth was not the place for Jesus to establish His base of ministry to the nation of Israel.

He Was Rejected by His Own

When Jesus returned to His hometown in the power of the Spirit to announce His ministry, the people were outraged. Luke 4:16-20 records the event: "And he came to Nazareth, where he had been brought up: and, as his custom was, he went into the synagogue on the sabbath day, and stood up for to read. And there was delivered unto him the book of the prophet Esaias. And when he had opened the book, he found the place where it was written, The Spirit of the Lord is upon me, because he hath anointed me to preach the gospel to the poor; he hath sent me to heal the broken-hearted, to preach deliverance to the captives, and recovering of sight to the blind, to set at liberty them that are bruised, to preach the acceptable year of the Lord. And he closed the book, and he gave it again to the minister, and sat down...."

It's important to note that when Jesus stood up to read this passage from Isaiah 61, He was not just reading text — He was making a prophetic proclamation. He was declaring from Scripture who He was. When the people of Nazareth sitting in the synagogue heard Him, they went from being shocked to being infuriated. In effect, they said, "Why, this is Joseph and Mary's son. We know all His sisters and brothers. Who in the world does He think He is? How dare He make such claims about Himself!"

Verse 20 goes on to say, "And the eyes of all them that were in the synagogue were fastened on him." The word "fastened" in the Greek is the same word used to describe *a viper who inserts its fangs into a victim*. The people of Nazareth wanted to sink their fangs into Jesus because of what He said. Luke 4:21 says, "And he began to say unto them, This day is this scripture fulfilled in your ears."

Jesus knew what the people were thinking and that they were gravely offended by what He had said. Thus, He said in verse 24, "Verily I say unto you, No prophet is accepted in his own country." Then Jesus uttered a few more indicting statements, the Bible says, "And all they in the synagogue, when they heard these things, were filled with wrath, and rose up, and thrust him out of the city, and led him unto the brow of the hill whereon their city was built, that they might cast him down headlong."

The people of Nazareth were so infuriated and offended at Jesus that they decided to kick Him out of town — by killing Him. However, through the supernatural protection of the Father, verse 30 says, "But he passing through the midst of them went his way, and came down to Capernaum, a city of Galilee, and taught them on the sabbath days."

Capernaum Was Spectacular

After being rejected and almost killed by the people of His hometown, Jesus went to Capernaum, and the differences between it and Nazareth were like night and day. Although Nazareth was small, close-minded, and unattractive, Capernaum was beautiful, open-minded, and rich in many ways. Located on the shores of the Sea of Galilee, Capernaum was a bustling city filled with many tourists, much trade, and a constant flow of travelers. It had one of the largest ports on the Sea of Galilee, which meant ships were coming and going, bringing fresh cargo and travelers regularly.

Capernaum was also home to a large regiment of Roman soldiers, including a centurion who requested and received healing from Jesus for his servant. There was also a major tax-collecting office in the city. This was the place where Jesus met and called Matthew, who was a tax collector. Because Capernaum was located near the border of Israel, many people passed through Capernaum to pay their taxes. When we combine the high level of trade, tourism, travelers, and tax collecting, Capernaum was a very wealthy city.

Another major advantage of being in Capernaum was its location on the Via Maris, which means *the way of the sea*. This was a major highway that ran from Damascus, just to the north of Israel, to Egypt in the south. So in addition to ships bringing people into the city, the Via Maris funneled them into Capernaum as well. People came from over the region around to enjoy the sea, have a great meal, and conduct business. Still today, Capernaum is situated on a major roadway that is built on top of the ancient Via Maris.

Indeed, Capernaum was totally different than Nazareth. In every way, it was a prosperous, affluent town, and it was in this very open, flourishing community that Jesus established His base of ministry. He relocated to a place where He would affect the most people. In fact, from His new home-town of Capernaum, He could impact the world.

Capernaum Became Known as the 'City of Jesus'

As a result of Capernaum's strategic location on the Via Maris and its large seaport, which brought in many tourists and travelers, news of Jesus' miraculous ministry traveled quickly even to remote regions. Interestingly, Jesus Himself became a major tourist attraction, and the city of Capernaum became known as the "city of Jesus." People from all over the region converged on the town of Capernaum to see Jesus and receive His healing touch. The truth is, more miracles happened in Capernaum than any other place in Israel.

Healings and Miracles Jesus Did in and Near Capernaum

- Jesus cast an unclean spirit out of a notable man in the synagogue, which is what launched His ministry from Capernaum (*see* Mark 1:21-28; Luke 4:32-37).

- Jesus healed Peter's mother-in-law of a fever (*see* Matthew 8:15; Mark 1:29-31; Luke 4:38, 39).

- Jesus healed many sick and demonized people (*see* Matthew 8:16; Mark 1:32-34; Luke 4:40-41).

- Jesus healed a leper (*see* Matthew 8:2-4; Mark 1:40-45; Luke 5:12-15).

- Jesus healed a paralytic (*see* Matthew 9:1-8; Mark 2:3-5; Luke 5:17-26).

- Jesus healed a man with a withered hand (*see* Matthew 12:10-13; Mark 3:1-5; Luke 6:6-10).

- Jesus healed the rich nobleman's son (*see* John 4:46-54).

- Jesus caused a miraculous catch of fish (*see* Luke 5:1-11).

- Jesus healed a centurion's servant (*see* Matthew 8:5-13; Luke 7:1-10).

- Jesus calmed the storm on the Sea of Galilee, just outside of Capernaum (*see* Matthew 8:23-27; Mark 4:35-41; Luke 8:22-25).

- Jesus healed the woman with the issue of blood (*see* Matthew 9:20-22; Mark 5:25-34; Luke 8:43-48).

- Jesus raised Jairus' daughter from the dead (*see* Matthew 9:18-26; Mark 5:22-43; Luke 8:41-56).

- Jesus healed two blind men and cast a mute spirit out of another man (*see* Matthew 9:27-31).

- Jesus walked on the Sea of Galilee, right near Capernaum (*see* Matthew 14:22-33; Mark 6:47-56; John 6:15-21).

- Jesus fed 4,000 people on a hillside, just outside of Capernaum (*see* Matthew 15:32-39; Mark 8:1-9).

- Jesus healed a boy who was under the influence of the occult (*see* Matthew 17:14-21).

- And Jesus performed the miracle of money in a fish's mouth (*see* Matthew 17:24-27).

A 'Tale' of Two Cities

As you read through the list of supernatural happenings, it is hard not to think about all that the people of Nazareth could have received but didn't. Why? It was all a result of their failure to accept Jesus for who He was — the Son of God. Their familiarity with Him and His family led to unbelief and offense, which shut down the power of God in their lives. Although Capernaum received an overflow of God's power, Nazareth barely saw a spark (*see* Matthew 13:54-58).

Capernaum welcomed Jesus with open arms. Nazareth threw Him out with clenched fists. Capernaum was open-minded, free, and accommodating. Nazareth was close-minded, religious, and resistant. The people of Capernaum made room for Jesus, and when you make room for Jesus, great things happen!

Peter made room for Jesus. As a resident of the city of Capernaum, he opened his home for the Master to use whenever He was in town. So Jesus stayed in Peter's home, and from Peter's home, the Lord's ministry was launched to all of Israel. You can still see the ruins of Peter's house in Capernaum today.

How about you? Will you make room for Jesus in your life? He is looking for those who will make space for Him so that He can release His miraculous power in and through them. If you open your heart and make

Him feel at home in you, He will release His miraculous ministry in and through your life too!

STUDY QUESTIONS

Study to shew thyself approved unto God, a workman that needeth not to be ashamed, rightly dividing the word of truth.
— 2 Timothy 2:15

1. What new insights did you learn about Jesus' hometown of *Nazareth*?
2. What fascinating facts did you discover about *Capernaum*, Jesus' base of ministry?
3. More miracles and healings took place in or near Capernaum than any other city in Israel. They were open and accommodating to Jesus, yet He spoke a strong word of judgment against them. What was it about them that caused Jesus to pronounce such a strong word (*see* Matthew 11:20-24; Luke 12:48)?

PRACTICAL APPLICATION

But be ye doers of the word, and not hearers only, deceiving your own selves.
— James 1:22

1. Jesus' move on to Capernaum was highly strategic. Its location allowed Him to make the greatest impact on the most people. How about you? Are you in the most effective place to make the greatest impact for His Kingdom? Has the Holy Spirit been prompting you to make a geographic change in where you live, work, or attend church?
2. The people in Nazareth had become too familiar with Jesus, which led to unbelief and offense that kept them from receiving His miraculous power. Have you become too familiar with Jesus? Do you see Him as ordinary, or as the extraordinary Son of God who is able to do exceedingly, abundantly more than you could ask or think? Pause and pray: "Holy Spirit, show me what's in my heart. Is there anything keeping me from receiving what You want to pour into my life?"

TOPIC

Jesus Casts an Unclean Spirit Out of a Notable Man

SCRIPTURES

1. **Mark 1:21-28** — And they went into Capernaum; and straightway on the sabbath day he entered into the synagogue, and taught. And they were astonished at his doctrine: for he taught them as one that had authority, and not as the scribes. And there was in their synagogue a man with an unclean spirit; and he cried out, saying, Let us alone; what have we to do with thee, thou Jesus of Nazareth? Art thou come to destroy us? I know who thou art, the Holy One of God. And Jesus rebuked him saying, Hold thy peace, and come out of him. And when the unclean spirit had torn him, and cried with a loud voice, he came out of him. And they were all amazed, insomuch that they questioned among themselves, saying, What thing is this? What new doctrine is this? For with authority commandeth he even the unclean spirits, and they do obey him. And immediately his fame spread abroad throughout all the region round about Galilee.

2. **John 1:14** — And the Word was made flesh, and dwelt among us....

GREEK WORDS

1. "taught"—**διδάσκω** (*didasko*): the tense means Jesus was teaching even as He entered the synagogue

2. "astonished"—**ἐκπλήσσω** (*ekplesso*): to be struck with astonishment; to be dumbfounded; to be at a loss for words

3. "had" — **ἔχω** (*echo*): to have, to hold, or to possess; the tense means holding something in one's possession

4. "authority" — **ἐξουσία** (*exousia*): authority or influence

5. "not" — **οὐχ** (*ouch*): emphatically no or emphatically not!

6. "scribes" — **γραμματεύς** (*grammateus*): describes a clerk, secretary, or scribe; used to describe a town clerk; theologian

7. "with a spirit" — ἐν πνεύματι (*en pneumati*): in the context of Mark 1:23, the man was in the grip of an unclean spirit; in the control of an unclean spirit

8. "unclean" — ἀκάθαρτος (*akathartos*): unclean, impure, filthy, lewd, or foul

9. "cried out" — ἀνακράζω (*anakradzo*): the tense means to repetitively scream or shriek

10. "saying"—λέγων (*legon*): saying repetitiously; indicates the spirit did not immediately submit, but argued with Jesus (Mark 1:24)

11. "destroy" — ἀπόλλυμι (*apollumi*): to undo; to destroy; to unravel; to disentangle; pictures something that is ruined, wasted, devastated; total destruction

12. "I know" — οἶδα (*oida*): pictures knowledge based on personal experience

13. "Holy One" — Ἅγιος (*Hagios*): in context, the Holy One

14. "rebuke"— ἐπιτιμάω (*epitimao*): to speak against; to insult or to humiliate; used in a court of law when a legal punishment was announced against a violator or lawbreaker

15. "hold thy peace" — φιμόω (*phimoo*): to be muzzled; to be silent; to be stilled

16. "out" — ἐξ (*ex*): out; it is where we get the word "exit"

17. "torn"—σπαράσσω (*sparasso*): to convulse; to throw into spasms, seizures, or violent tremors

18. "amazed"— θαμβέω (*thambeo*): dumbfounded to the point of shutting down

19. "new" — καινός (*kainos*): new; unprecedented; novel

20. "commandeth" — ἐπιτάσσω (*epitasso*): a military term to denote the authoritative voice of a commander who gives the charge for disorder to become ordered

21. "even" — καὶ (*kai*): even; describes an emphatic statement; portrays a sense of amazement and shock

22. "obey" — ὑπακούω (*hupakouo*): to fall in line; to obey what is spoken

23. "fame"— ἀκοή (*akoe*): pictures the ear; something heard; a widespread rumor; news ringing in the ears

SYNOPSIS

The city of Capernaum — also known as the "city of Jesus" — was a very strategic location. It was situated on a major thoroughfare called the Via Maris, which ran from Egypt in the south to Damascus in the north. This well-to-do fishing village anchored on the shores of the Sea of Galilee became Jesus' ministry base after He left Nazareth. It's interesting to note that the majority of His notable miracles were done in Capernaum. This includes the deliverance of a demon-possessed man who was in the synagogue the day Jesus first came to town.

The emphasis of this lesson:

The moment Jesus entered Capernaum, the healings began. His authority and power were displayed in ways the people had never before seen. When He delivered the man from the unclean spirit, His fame rapidly spread throughout the region.

Jesus' Grand Entrance Into Capernaum

Mark 1:21 says, "And they went into Capernaum; and straightway on the sabbath day he entered into the synagogue, and taught." The word "taught" is the Greek word *didasko*, which refers to *a systematic teaching*. The form of *didasko* used here means *He entered the synagogue teaching*. He didn't wait until they gave Him the podium. He was already elaborating on the Word of God as He walked through the door.

Remember, Jesus is the Word made flesh (*see* John 1:14). He was "the walking Bible." Everywhere He went, He was constantly unpacking the revelation of Scripture. It's who He is, and that is what He was doing as He walked into the synagogue in Capernaum.

Mark 1:22 says, "And they were astonished at his doctrine: for he taught them as one that had authority, and not as the scribes." The word "astonished" is the Greek word *ekplesso*, which means *to be struck with astonishment; to be dumbfounded; to be at a loss of words; to gasp in astonishment*. The religious people who regularly attended the synagogue in Capernaum had never heard such teaching. They were astonished at His "doctrine," which is the Greek word *didasko*, and it refers to *systematic teaching; reliable, time-tested doctrine*.

The verse goes on to say that Jesus taught them as One who "had authority." The word "had" is a form of the Greek word *echo*, which means *I have; I hold; I possess*. The form used here literally means *as one having authority*. Therefore, you could literally translate it *to have, to hold, to possess, or to be in actual possession of a thing*.

What was Jesus holding in His possession? The Scripture says "authority," which is the Greek word *exousia*, and it means *authority or influence*. Both Jesus and Paul used this word throughout the New Testament. Jesus had in His possession *real authority that had been entrusted to Him by the Father*.

Mark explicitly says the authority Jesus had was "not as the scribes." The word "not" is the Greek word *ouch*, which means *emphatically no* or *emphatically not!* Of all the Greek words used for not, *ouch* is the strongest. Jesus was *emphatically not like the scribes*. His words were packed with supernatural power, not just information.

The "scribes" refers to those who were committed to doctrine and who meticulously copied each letter and verse of the law. They were highly intellectual people who literally made copies of the Scriptures. Although they exuded much intellectual activity, Jesus imparted dynamic power and authority.

He Encountered a Man With an Unclean Spirit

Immediately upon entering a room, there was an instantaneous spiritual reaction to Jesus' authority. This is not clearly seen in the text of the *King James Version*, but it is seen in the original Greek text of Mark 1:23. "And there was in their synagogue a man with an unclean spirit; and he cried out."

Notice it says, "...A man with an unclean spirit." The phrase "with a spirit" is the Greek phrase *en pneumati*, and it doesn't mean the man was in possession of an unclean spirit. On the contrary, it means *the man was in the grip or control of an unclean spirit*. Thus, it could be translated, "And there was in their synagogue a man in the grip of — a man completely in the control of — an unclean spirit."

Also note the word "unclean." It is the Greek word *akathartos*, and it means *to be unclean, impure, filthy, lewd, or foul*. To those in the synagogue, this man likely appeared normal. They could not see the morally lewd spirit that was controlling his thinking, and possibly his actions, in private. Yet the spirit was there, and when Jesus walked into the synagogue teaching with supernatural authority and power, the unclean spirit "cried out."

This phrase "cried out" is the Greek word *anakradzo*, and the tense of this word means *to repetitively scream or shriek*. This man released a prolonged, bloodcurdling scream. The unclean spirit — the demon in control of the man — panicked and began to disrupt what was taking place when Christ entered.

What Did the Unclean Spirit Scream?

Mark 1:24 indicates that the spirit was saying, "...Let us alone; what have we to do with thee, thou Jesus of Nazareth? Art thou come to destroy us? I know who thou art, the Holy One of God." First, notice the word "saying." It is the Greek word *legon*, which means *to repetitiously say something*. This indicates that the demon kept screaming and shrieking words of panic in the presence of everyone.

"Art thou come to destroy us?" was one of the things the unclean spirit screamed. The word "destroy" is a translation of the Greek word *apollumi*. It is from the words *lumi*, meaning *to unloose*, and the word *apo*, which means *away from*. When these two words are compounded to form *apollumi*, it means *to undo; to destroy; to unravel; to disentangle*. It pictures something that is *ruined, wasted,* or *devastated; total destruction*. Basically, the demon asked Jesus, "Did You come to untie and disentangle us from this man and utterly destroy us?"

The unclean spirit then said, "I know who thou art, the Holy One of God" (v. 24). The phrase "I know" is a translation of the Greek word *oida*, which describes *knowledge gained by personal experience*. This demon had personal experience with Jesus in the past. He was familiar with Jesus from when Satan had attempted to exalt his throne above God's (*see* Ezekiel 28). In that moment of Satan's rebellion against God, the Bible says Jesus cast him and all the rebellious angels out of Heaven.

The unclean spirit knew Jesus from personal experience as "the Holy One of God." The words "Holy One" is the Greek word *Hagios*. In the Greek context of this verse, the H is capitalized, indicating Jesus is not just *a* holy person; He is *THE Holy One of God*.

How Did Jesus Respond to the Unclean Spirit?

Mark 1:25 says, "And Jesus rebuked him saying, Hold thy peace, and come out of him." Again, we see the word "saying," which is the Greek word *legon*, meaning *to say something repetitiously*. This tells us that the unclean spirit didn't immediately respond and submit, but instead, argued with Jesus.

At once, Jesus "rebuked" the spirit. "Rebuked" is the Greek word *epitimao*, and it means *to speak against; to insult or to humiliate*. It was a word used in a court of law when a legal punishment was announced against a violator or lawbreaker. When Jesus "rebuked" the demon, He pronounced a verdict of judgment on him.

Then He told it to "hold thy peace," which is the Greek word *phimoo*, meaning *to be muzzled; to be silent; to be stilled*. When this demonic spirit was screeching and screaming his words of fear, Jesus told it to shut up and come "out." The word "out" is the Greek word *ex*, which is where we get the word *exit*. Jesus demanded the demon exit the man immediately.

How the Unclean Spirit and the People Reacted

Mark 1:26 tells us how the unclean spirit reacted to Jesus' command. "And when the unclean spirit had torn him, and cried with a loud voice, he came out of him." The word "torn" is the Greek word *sparasso*, which means *to convulse; to throw into spasms, seizures, or violent tremors*. It can even be translated *to mangle*.

When Jesus demanded the demon to exit the man, it threw him into violent spasms or seizures. The man was convulsing and gasping in response to the unclean spirit's departure.

Verse 27 says, "And they were all amazed, insomuch that they questioned among themselves, saying, What thing is this? What new doctrine is this? For with authority commandeth he even the unclean spirits, and they do obey him."

The people in the synagogue were "amazed" — the Greek word *thambeo*, which means *to be dumbfounded to the point of emotionally shutting down*. When they saw how Jesus handled this demonic spirit, they were virtually speechless. They didn't know how to respond. All they could muster was, "What thing is this? What new doctrine is this?" The word "new" is the

Greek word *kainos*, which describes *something new, unprecedented, or novel*. These people had never seen anything like this.

They continued saying, "For with authority commandeth he even the unclean spirits, and they do obey him." The word "commandeth" is the Greek word *epitasso*, which is *a military term to denote the authoritative voice of a commander who gives the charge for disorder to become ordered*. And the word "obey" is the Greek word *hupakouo*, which is also a military term meaning *to fall in line or to obey what is spoken*.

When Jesus, the Commander-in-Chief of Heaven's armies, told the unclean spirit to exit, the people essentially said, "Even the unclean spirits fall in line to His authority." The word "even" is the Greek word *kai*, and it is *an emphatic statement that portrays a sense of amazement and shock*. Again, we see the sense of awe that came upon the people.

Once Jesus had miraculously delivered this man, Mark 1:28 informs us that, "...Immediately his fame spread abroad throughout all the region round about Galilee." The word "fame" is the Greek word *akoe*, and it is the Greek word for "the ear." It describes *something that is heard; a widespread rumor or spreading of information*. It is the picture of *news ringing in the ears of its hearers*. The news of what Jesus did began to travel throughout the whole region. People were talking about the Miracle Worker who had moved to the city of Capernaum, and the "buzz" created by their reports launched Jesus into His miracle ministry in the city of Capernaum.

STUDY QUESTIONS

> **Study to shew thyself approved unto God, a workman that needeth not to be ashamed, rightly dividing the word of truth.**
> — 2 Timothy 2:15

1. After hearing about Jesus' encounter with the man with the unclean spirit, what new insights have you gained?
2. Jesus had great authority, and the people of Capernaum could clearly see it. What did Jesus say about His authority in Matthew 28:18-20 and Luke 10:19 and 20? What are some of the signs of His authority depicted in Mark 16:17 and 18?
3. Who in your life walks in obvious godly authority? What do you attribute to this person's ability to walk in this place of spiritual authority?

PRACTICAL APPLICATION

> But be ye doers of the word, and not hearers only,
> deceiving your own selves.
> — James 1:22

1. Although the people of Nazareth were religious, small-minded, and closed to Jesus, the residents of Capernaum were open, accommodating, and welcoming. Nazareth missed out on Jesus' power, and Capernaum experienced it. Which city are you more like? What evidence in your life confirms your answer?

2. Does it surprise you to hear that a man attending "church" had an unclean spirit controlling his life? What about this scenario is most alarming to you? Why?

3. What aspects of Jesus' authority are you most passionate to see released in you and in others? Take a moment now to pray. Ask the Lord to show you anything that is keeping you from seeing His power at work, and invite Him to have His way in your life.

LESSON 3

TOPIC

Jesus Heals Peter's Mother-in-Law

SCRIPTURES

1. **Mark 1:29-34** — And forthwith, when they were come out of the synagogue, they entered into the house of Simon and Andrew, with James and John. But Simon's wife's mother lay sick of a fever, and anon they tell him of her. And he came and took her by the hand, and lifted her up; and immediately the fever left her, and she ministered unto them. And at even, when the sun did set, they brought unto him all that were diseased, and them that were possessed with devils. And all the city was gathered together at the door. And he healed many that were sick of divers diseases, and cast out many devils; and suffered not the devils to speak, because they knew him.

GREEK WORDS

1. "amazed" — θαμβέω (*thambeo*): dumbfounded to the point of shutting down

2. "commandeth" — ἐπιτάσσω (*epitasso*): a military term to denote the authoritative voice of a commander who gives the charge for disorder to become ordered

3. "even" — καὶ (*kai*): even; describes an emphatic statement; portrays a sense of amazement and shock

4. "obey" — ὑπακούω (*hupakouo*): to fall in line; to obey what is spoken

5. "fame" — ἀκοή (*akoe*): pictures the ear; something heard; a widespread rumor; news ringing in the ears

6. "lay sick" — κατάκειμαι (*katakeimai*): to lie down; lying down due to sickness

7. "fever" — πυρέσσουσα (*puressousa*): pictures a fiery, scorching heat; the tense means she was feverish, suffering from a prolonged, fiery fever

8. "took" — κρατέω (*krateo*): to seize; to firmly grip; to apprehend; taking something by force; pictures a masterful grip

9. "left" — ἀφίημι (*aphiemi*): to dismiss, release, discharge; to send away; in this case, the fever was dismissed, discharged, and sent away, and she was liberated from that feverish condition

10. "ministered" — διακονέω (*diakoneo*): to serve like a high-level servant; pictures serving that is honorable and done in a way as to make people feel like nobility; professional serving

11. "diseased"(v.32),"sick"(v.34) — κακῶς ἔχοντας (*kakosechontas*): anyone in bad shape or in a bad condition; anyone having anything wrong with him

12. "all" — πάντας (*pantas*): everyone, no one excluded

13. "being possessed with devils" — δαιμονίζομαι (*daimonidzomai*): demonized; pictures those under the influence of a demon or group of demons; the tense indicates a chronic case of demonization

14. "healed" — θεραπεύω (*therapeuo*): pictures a healing touch that requires corresponding actions; therapy

15. "many" — πολλοὺς (*pollous*): the plural form of πολύς (*polus*), meaning a great number or multitudes

16. "diseases" — νόσος (*nosos*): a terminal condition for which there is no natural cure; spirit-induced illnesses, physical or mental; medical

attempts to treat such illnesses were considered futile; it was assumed that anyone with this type of disease had no hope of recuperation; an unalterable, irreversible, incurable, permanent condition

17. "cast out" — ἐκβάλλω (*ekballo*): to forcibly evict; to throw out; to cast out; to expel; to drive out; to kick out; to cast out; historically, it was used to describe a nation that forcibly deported lawbreakers from its borders

18. "to speak" — λαλέω (*laleo*): to speak; to talk; to converse

SYNOPSIS

The house of the apostle Peter was located in the city of Capernaum. It was identified in the Fourth Century by a prominent Christian who came to the city and recorded that the house's walls were still intact and had been used to construct a church. Even today, a Catholic Church is built directly over the site where Peter's First-Century home once stood. It was in this house that scores of miracles took place, starting with the healing of Peter's mother-in-law, who was very sick with a fever.

The emphasis of this lesson:

Immediately after delivering the man with the unclean spirit, Jesus went to Peter's house and healed his mother-in-law from a lingering fever. Within hours, He was touching and healing the sick from all over the city. No disease or demon could stand against Him.

Jesus Displayed Unprecedented Authority

When Jesus arrived in Capernaum, Mark 1:21 says He went "straightway" to the synagogue and began teaching. The word "straightway" means *without pause, without delay,* or *immediately.* In other words, Jesus didn't waste any time getting down to business.

Mark 1:22 says, "And they were astonished at his doctrine: for he taught them as one that had authority, and not as the scribes." We saw in the last lesson that the word "astonished" is the Greek word *ekplesso,* which means *to be struck with astonishment; to be dumbfounded; to be at a loss for words.* The people in the synagogue were gasping in astonishment upon hearing His doctrine.

These people had heard much teaching over the years, but they had not heard it with the bold level of authority in which Jesus presented it. Mark

1:22 says, "…For he taught as one that had authority.…" We learned that the word "had" is a form of the Greek word *echo*, and it means *having authority; possessing authority; or having authority in his possession.*

Clearly, Jesus had real authority, "not as the scribes." The word "not" is the Greek word *ouch*, which means *emphatically not!* To be clear, the scribes held an important position as scriptural technicians that ensured God's Word was accurately written down. But they didn't have the spiritual power of Jesus. It was His supernatural power and authority that dumbfounded the people.

Nowhere To Hide From His Presence

As Jesus was teaching, Mark 1:23 says, "There was in their synagogue a man with an unclean spirit; and he cried out." We discovered that the original Greek rendering of this verse says the man was "in the grip of" or "in the control of" an unclean spirit. And the word "unclean" is the Greek word *akathartos*, which means *unclean, impure, filthy, lewd, or foul.*

Right in the middle of the synagogue, underneath all of this man's religious garb, an unclean spirit was operating. It was a *sexually and morally lewd spirit.* When it heard Jesus teaching with authority, it began screeching and screaming, "…Let us alone; what have we to do with thee, thou Jesus of Nazareth? Art thou come to destroy us? I know who thou art, the Holy One of God" (Mark 1:24).

We learned that the word "destroy" is the Greek word *apollumi*, which means *to undo; to unravel; to disentangle; to disengage.* It pictures *total destruction* or something that is *ruined, wasted,* or *devastated.* The unclean spirit was literally saying, "Did You come to undo and disentangle me from this man and totally destroy me?"

That wasn't the only thing the demon screamed. He also yelled, "…I know who thou art, the Holy One of God." The phrase "I know" is from the Greek word *oida*, which describes *knowledge based on personal experience.* By using this word, it was as if the unclean spirit was saying, "Based on my past experience with You, Jesus, there are some things I know about You."

The last encounter the unclean spirit had experienced with Jesus was likely when Lucifer (Satan) attempted to exalt his throne above God's throne, and he and the angels that rebelled with him were evicted from Heaven (*see* Ezekiel 28:12-17). This evil spirit knew from experience that Jesus was in the unraveling and evicting business, and he knew that he was about to be kicked out of this man.

Jesus Demanded the Demon to Make an Exit

Immediately, the Scripture says, "Jesus rebuked him saying, Hold thy peace, and come out of him" (Mark 1:25). The phrase "hold thy peace" is the Greek word *phimoo*, which means *to be muzzled; to be silent; to be stilled*. Basically, Jesus told the demon to shut up and get out. The word "out" in verse 25 is the Greek word *ex*, which means *exit*.

The Bible says, "...When the unclean spirit had torn him, and cried with a loud voice, he came out of him. And they were all amazed, insomuch that they questioned among themselves, saying, What thing is this? What new doctrine is this?" (vv. 26, 27). The people in the synagogue were dumbfounded by what they saw. To them it was a "new" doctrine. The word "new" is the Greek word *kainos*, which describes *something unprecedented* or *previously not known*.

The people added, "...For with authority commandeth he even the unclean spirits, and they do obey him" (v. 27). We saw that the word "even" is the Greek word *kai*, which is *an emphatic statement; it portrays a sense of amazement and shock*. Essentially, the people in the synagogue exclaimed, "Wow! Jesus has so much authority that *even* unclean spirits obey Him."

Peter's Mother-in-Law Was Very Sick

After miraculously delivering the man with the unclean spirit, Jesus made His way to Peter's house in the city Capernaum. Mark 1:29 and 30 says, "And forthwith, when they were come out of the synagogue, they entered into the house of Simon and Andrew, with James and John. But Simon's wife's mother lay sick of a fever, and anon they tell him of her."

Notice it says Peter's mother-in-law "lay sick." This is the Greek word *katakeimai*, and it is *the picture of someone lying down due to sickness*. This woman was so sick with "fever" that she couldn't get out of bed. The word "fever" is the Greek word *puressousa*, and it indicates *a fiery, scorching heat; the tense means she was feverish, suffering from a prolonged, fiery fever*. In the ancient world, a consuming fever of this nature was serious and could prove fatal.

Accordingly, Jesus "came and took her by the hand, and lifted her up; and immediately the fever left her, and she ministered unto them" (Mark 1:31). The phrase "took her by the hand" is quite remarkable. The word "took" is a form of the Greek word *krateo*, which means *to seize; to firmly grip; to apprehend*. It indicates *taking something by force*. It pictures a *masterful grip*. This tells us that when Jesus "took" Peter's mother-in-law by the hand, He didn't gently touch her. He aggressively seized her hand. His actions indicate that He was forcefully attacking the sickness and releasing His faith.

While she was still in the grips of disease, Jesus lifted this woman up, "and immediately the fever left her." The word "left" is a form of the Greek word *aphiemi*, which means *to dismiss, release, discharge; to send away*. In this case, the fever was dismissed, discharged, and sent away, and Peter's mother-in-law was instantaneously set free from that lingering feverish condition.

Once she was healed, the Scripture says "she ministered unto them." The word "ministered" is a form of the Greek word *diakoneo*, which means *to serve like a high-level servant; serving that is honorable and done in a way as to make people feel like nobility; professional serving*. Thus, she was radically healed and immediately began to express her appreciation to Jesus by serving Him and His companions.

It's interesting to note that Jesus didn't pray *for* her. In fact, nowhere in any of the four gospels does it say that Jesus prayed *for* the sick. It says He *spoke to* the sick, He *touched* the sick, and He *took authority over* sickness. When He released His faith, people were healed.

Jesus Healed a Steady Stream of Sick People

Mark 1:32 says, "And at even, when the sun did set, they brought unto him all that were diseased, and them that were possessed with devils." The word "brought" is the Greek word *phero*, and it means *to physically carry*. These people were so sick they needed to be carried to where Jesus was. The tense of the word *phero* indicates there was a steady stream of critically ill people being carried to Christ.

We also see that these people were "diseased," which is the Greek word *kakos echontas*. *Echontas* is from the word *echo*, which means *to have*, and the word *kakos* describes *something evil, vile, foul, or bad*. When the two words are compounded to form *kakos echontas* — here translated "diseased" — it indicates *anyone in bad shape or in a bad condition; anyone having anything wrong with him*.

"All that were diseased" were brought to Jesus. The word "all" is the Greek word *pantas*, and it means *everyone, no one excluded*. This included "them that were possessed with devils." The phrase "possessed with devils" is the Greek word *daimonidzomai*, which means *those that were demonized; those under the influence of a demon or group of demons*. The tense here indicates *a chronic case of demonization*.

How many showed up at Peter's house for healing? "And *all the city* was gathered together at the door" (Mark 1:33). What did Jesus do for the crowds pressing in to touch Him? Verse 34 says, "And he healed many that were sick of divers diseases, and cast out many devils . . . ."

The word "healed" is the Greek word *therapeuo*. It is where we get the word *therapy*, and *it pictures a healing touch that requires corresponding actions*. In other words, Jesus didn't just touch people and send them on their way. He required them to do something to demonstrate that they were healed. If the person had a withered hand, He commanded them to stretch it forth. If they couldn't walk and were confined to a mat, He told them to pick up their mat and walk. In all the gospels, the word *therapeuo* is the word most often used to describe the healing ministry of Jesus.

Mark 1:34 states that Jesus healed "many" that were "sick." The word "many" is the Greek word *pollous*, meaning *a great number or multitudes*. Thus, there was a huge crowd of "sick" people that showed up at Peter's house. Again, this word "sick" is the Greek words *kakos echontas*, and it describes *anyone in bad shape or in a bad condition; anyone having anything wrong with him*.

Jesus healed many that were sick of "divers diseases." Here the word "diseases" is the Greek word *nosos*, which denotes *a terminal condition for which there is no natural cure; spirit-induced illnesses, physical or mental. Medical attempts to treat such illnesses were considered futile; it was assumed that anyone with this type of disease had no hope of recuperation; it was an unalterable, irreversible, incurable, permanent condition*.

These were the types of "diseases" that Jesus was healing. What was considered incurable and irreversible by society was totally curable for Jesus. In fact, the Bible says He "cast out many devils." The phrase "cast out" is the Greek word *ekballo*, which means *to forcibly evict; to throw out; to cast out; to expel; to drive out; to kick out*. Historically, this word was used to describe *a nation that forcibly deported lawbreakers from its borders*.

Jesus evicted many devils from those that were sick. With supernatural authority He "suffered not the devils to speak, because they knew him." The phrase "to speak" is the Greek term *laleo*, and it means *to speak; to talk; to converse.* Just like the unclean spirit that was controlling the man in the synagogue, the demons in these sick people wanted to speak out. But Jesus wouldn't allow them. He boldly told them to shut up and come out.

When the demons left, the people recovered their health. The problems they were dealing with were not physical; they were spiritual. When the spiritual problems were addressed, the physical problems were remedied.

STUDY QUESTIONS

Study to shew thyself approved unto God, a workman that needeth not to be ashamed, rightly dividing the word of truth.
— 2 Timothy 2:15

1. What new things did you learn about Jesus and the multiple miracles Jesus did at Peter's house in Capernaum? (*See* Mark 1:30-34.)

2. Just as Jesus wasted no time in getting to work in the lives of the people in Capernaum, He desires to get to work in your life too. Take a few moments to chew on the words of Isaiah 43:18 and 19. What area(s) of your life would you say God is at work like this? What is He doing? Also consider Isaiah 48:6 and Revelation 21:5.

PRACTICAL APPLICATION

But be ye doers of the word, and not hearers only, deceiving your own selves.
—James 1:22

When Peter's mother-in-law was healed of the lingering feverish condition, she was extremely grateful and immediately began to express her appreciation to Jesus by ministering to Him.

1. Think back on your life's journey. From what lingering condition or situation has the Lord healed or delivered you? Why were you grateful?

2. Have you asked Jesus, "Lord, what can I do for You? How can I best serve Your needs to express my appreciation?" If you have, what did He ask you to do? It you haven't, why not take a moment now to ask Him what He would have you do.

TOPIC

Jesus Heals a Nobleman's Son

SCRIPTURES

1. **John 4:46-54** — So Jesus came again into Cana of Galilee, where he made the water wine. And there was a certain nobleman, whose son was sick at Capernaum. When he heard that Jesus was come out of Judaea into Galilee, he went unto him, and besought him that he would come down, and heal his son: for he was at the point of death. Then said Jesus unto him, Except ye see signs and wonders, ye will not believe. The nobleman saith unto him, Sir, come down ere my child die. Jesus saith unto him, Go thy way; thy son liveth. And the man believed the word that Jesus had spoken unto him, and he went his way. And as he was now going down, his servants met him, and told him, saying, Thy son liveth. Then inquired he of them the hour when he began to amend. And they said unto him, Yesterday at the seventh hour the fever left him. So the father knew that it was at the same hour, in which Jesus said unto him, Thy son liveth: and himself believed, and his whole house. This is again the second miracle that Jesus did, when he was come out of Judaea into Galilee.

GREEK WORDS

1. "nobleman" — βασιλικὸς (*basilikos*): royalty; nobility; pictures a prince, possibly a Jewish prince or even Roman nobility

2. "son" — υἱός (*huios*): son; in this case, a future royal inheritor

3. "sick" — ἀσθενέω (*astheneo*): pictures one feeble or frail in health; fragile, faint, incapacitated, or disabled; one in such poor health that he would be difficult to transport

4. "besought" — ἐρωτάω (*erotao*): to fervently demand; pictures a strong request; the tense conveys an incessant appeal

5. "heal" — ἰάομαι (*iaomai*): to cure; to progressively reverse a condition; often denotes healing that comes to pass over a period of time; depicts sickness that has been progressively healed rather than instantaneously healed

6. "at the point of death"(v. 47), "die"(v. 49) — ἀποθνήσκω (*apothnesko*): to wither away; to waste away; to slowly die; to gradually die

7. "signs" — σημεῖον (*semeion*): used in the Gospels primarily to depict miracles and supernatural events

8. "wonders"— τέρας (*teras*): something that baffles, bewilders, astonishes, and leaves one at a loss of words; shock, surprise, or astonishment felt by bystanders who observed events that were contrary to the normal course of nature; miraculous events so shocking, they left people speechless, bewildered, baffled, stunned, and in a state of wonder

9. "Sir" — Κύριε (*Kurie*): a recognition of Christ's power, lordship, and mastery (v. 49)

10. "child" — παιδίον (*paidion*): a child under parental authority

11. "Go thy way"(v. 50), "went his way"(v. 50) — πορεύομαι (*poreuomai*): to go on a journey; to be on your way; communicates, "it's time for you to be on your journey"; get going; get moving

12. "believed"— ἐπίστευσεν (*episteusen*): depicts a faith that is released at a precise moment

13. "son" — παῖς (*pais*): small boy; a young child

14. "liveth" — ζάω (*dzao*): full of life; no longer lifeless or dying

15. "inquired"—πυνθάνομαι (*punthanomai*): to learn by asking questions; to inquire; "give me evidence" or "give me facts"

16. "amend" — κομψότερον (*kompsoteron*): well-dressed; to be bettered

17. "whole house"— ὅλος (*holos*): whole; complete; entire; it is where we get the word "wholeness"

18. "did" — ποιέω (*poieo*): to make; to create; carries the idea of creativity

SYNOPSIS

The city of Capernaum was Jesus' ministry base, and many notable miracles happened in and near there. For instance, there was a nobleman from Capernaum whose son had become deathly sick, but when he learned that Jesus was nearby in Cana, he swiftly left where he was and sought out Jesus to heal his boy. This is the story of the boy's miraculous healing and the salvation of his whole family.

The emphasis of this lesson:

The second miracle that Jesus did when He came into Galilee was healing the sick son of a nobleman from Capernaum. In addition to the

son's miraculous healing, the nobleman and his whole house surrendered their lives to the Lordship of Jesus.

Meet the Nobleman and His Son

Capernaum was the leading city in Galilee at the time of Christ's ministry. It was a very prosperous border town with a thriving fishing industry, abundant travelers and tourists, a strong military base, a tax-collection center, and a very large synagogue. Not only did many people come in and out of Capernaum, there were also a number of wealthy nobility living there. This brings us to a story that begins in John 4:46.

> **So Jesus came again into Cana of Galilee, where he made the water wine. And there was a certain nobleman, whose son was sick at Capernaum.**

First, notice the word "nobleman" — the Greek word *basilikos*. It is taken from the Greek word *basileuos*, which is the Greek term for a *king*. *Basilikos* describes *royalty or nobility*. It pictures *a prince, possibly a Jewish prince or even royal nobility*. Capernaum was a high-level, affluent town, so it is no surprise that someone of royalty or nobility would be living there.

Verse 46 also discloses that this nobleman's "son" was sick. The word "son" is the Greek word *huios*, which describes *a son, and in this particular case, a future royal inheritor*. The word "sick" is the Greek word *astheneo*, which pictures *one feeble or frail in health; fragile, faint, incapacitated, or disabled; one in such poor health that he would be difficult to transport*.

The sickness with which the nobleman's son was afflicted was "fever," which is the Greek word indicating *a scorching fiery heat; a fever that is prolonged and can't be brought under control*. This fever was very similar to the one Peter's mother-in-law had. Fevers were quite serious and even fatal at that time.

The Nobleman Sought Out Jesus

John 4:47 says, "When he [the nobleman] heard that Jesus was come out of Judaea into Galilee, he went unto him, and besought him that he would come down, and heal his son: for he was at the point of death." As soon as this man heard Jesus was nearby, he quickly went to see Him and "besought" Him.

The word "besought" is the Greek word *erotao*, which means *to fervently demand*. It pictures *a strong request*, and the tense used conveys the idea of *an incessant appeal*. The nobleman placed a strong demand on Jesus to come at once to heal his son, expecting Jesus to respond in a positive way, which we know He did.

The word "heal" used in verse 47 is the Greek word *iaomai*, and it means *to cure*. What makes *iaomai* unique from other Greek words for "healing" is that it means *to progressively reverse a condition*. It often denotes healing that comes to pass over a period of time. It depicts *sickness that has been progressively healed rather than instantaneously healed*. Along with the gift of the working of miracles, which happen instantaneously, the Holy Spirit also provides us with the gifts of "healing" (*iaomai*) — the progressive, day-by-day recovery in which one grows stronger and stronger (*see* 1 Corinthians 12:9-11).

By using this word, we can determine the nobleman's level of faith. He wasn't asking for instantaneous results. He just believed that if Jesus would come and speak a word of healing, his son would begin to fully recover. His son's condition was serious, "for he was at the point of death."

The phrase "he was" is the Greek word *mello*, which means *he was about to arrive at the point of death*. The Greek word for "at the point of death" is *apothnesko*, and it literally means *to wither away; to waste away; to slowly die; to gradually die*. This father was saying, "My son is dying right before my eyes — he's wasting away day by day, losing weight and becoming weaker and weaker." Scripture says "he was" at the point of death. Indeed, this was a critical situation.

It took great faith and humility for this powerful man of nobility to seek out Jesus. Nevertheless, he was desperate. His son — likely the heir to his position — was at death's door. Therefore, he laid aside his dignity, his status, and his wealth and fervently demanded Jesus to come down and heal his boy.

Jesus and the Nobleman Converse

In John 4:48, Jesus said to him, "...Except ye see signs and wonders, ye will not believe." On the surface, Jesus' response may seem like a rebuke, but it wasn't. Here, Jesus was acknowledging that He understood the human need to see the power of God demonstrated in order for faith to be ignited. A better translation of this verse in the Greek would be, "*Unless* you see signs and wonders, you will not believe."

The word "signs" is the Greek word *semeion*, and it is used in the gospels primarily to depict *miracles and supernatural events*. The word "wonders" is the Greek word *teras*, and it describes *something that baffles, bewilders, astonishes, and leaves one at a loss of words*. The word "wonders" is actually not a second category of supernatural activity; it is the people's response to the "signs." Therefore, Jesus' words in this passage could be better translated, "Unless you see signs that baffle and signs that cause wonder, it's difficult for you to believe." This is why we need the power of God displayed as we evangelize and share the message of Christ.

John 4:49 says, "The nobleman saith unto him, Sir, come down ere my child die." Notice, he addressed Jesus as "Sir." This is the Greek word *Kurie*, which is a form of the word *kurios*, and it means *lord or master*. It is a recognition of Christ's power, lordship, and mastery. In that moment, the nobleman recognized Jesus as Lord of the situation with his son. He said, in effect, "Lord, Master, I'm submitting to You. I know You are the only One who can change what I'm dealing with. Come down or my son will die." The word "die" is the Greek word *apothnesko* — the same word translated "death" earlier. It means *to wither away; to waste away; to slowly die; to gradually die*.

Jesus Answered the Nobleman's Request

"Jesus saith unto him, Go thy way; thy son liveth. And the man believed the word that Jesus had spoken unto him, and he went his way" (John 4:50). The phrase "Go thy way" is the Greek word *poreuomai*, and it means *to go on a journey; to be on your way*. A better translation would be, "*Get going; get moving.*"

Why did Jesus tell him to "get moving"? The reason was that his "son liveth." The word "liveth" is the Greek word *dzao*, which means *full of life; full of vitality; no longer lifeless or dying*. Upon hearing these words, "the man believed the words Jesus had spoken." The word "believed" is the Greek word *episteusen*, and it depicts *a faith that is released at a precise moment*. The instant the nobleman heard Jesus say that his son "liveth," he didn't argue or question. He believed the word Jesus spoke and claimed it.

The Bible says, "He went on his way." The Greek tense of this phrase indicates he quickly or immediately "got moving" and headed for home. "And as he was now going down, his servants met him, and told him, saying, Thy son liveth" (John 4:51). The word "saying" in Greek means *to repetitiously say something.* In other words, the nobleman's servants were so excited that the boy was recovering, they kept saying it again and again: "Your son is alive! He's turned the corner! Your son liveth!" Again, the word "liveth" is the Greek word *dzao*, meaning *full of life; no longer lifeless or dying.*

Immediately, the nobleman "...inquired he of them the hour when he began to amend. And they said unto him, Yesterday at the seventh hour the fever left him" (John 4:52). The word "inquired" is the Greek word *punthanomai*, and it means *to learn by asking questions; to inquire.* It's the equivalent of saying, *"Give me evidence,"* or *"Give me facts."* He wanted to know when and where the healing occurred.

Specifically, the man asked to know "when he began to amend." The word "amend" is the Greek word *kompsoteron*, which means *to be well-dressed.* This lets us know that the child was no longer lying flat on his back with fever. He was up, well-dressed, and getting around nicely. The fever had "left." The word "left" is the Greek word *aphiemi*, which means *to permanently leave* or *permanently be dismissed.* When the fever left the boy, it never came back, and it went away at about the seventh hour.

Verse 53 says, "So the father knew that it was at the same hour, in which Jesus said unto him, Thy son liveth: and himself believed, and his whole house." The word "whole" is the Greek word *holos*, meaning *whole; complete;* or *entire.* It is where we get the word "wholeness." Remarkably, the nobleman and his entire household believed in Jesus that day and received "wholeness."

John 4:54 tells us, "This is again the second miracle that Jesus did, when he was come out of Judaea into Galilee." The word "did" is the Greek word *poieo*, which means *to make* or *to create.* It always carries the idea of *creativity.* Jesus released creative power in the life of the nobleman's son. He did what could not be done in the natural. With the power of His spoken word, He not only healed the boy of sickness, He changed the eternal destiny of the entire family.

STUDY QUESTIONS

Study to shew thyself approved unto God, a workman that needeth not to be ashamed, rightly dividing the word of truth.
— 2 Timothy 2:15

1. When you pray, how do you normally approach God? Carefully read Ephesians 3:12 and Hebrews 4:16 and describe how God wants you to come to Him. Also consider Hebrews 10:19-22.

2. When the nobleman learned from his servants that his son had been healed the exact moment Jesus had spoken the word, how did he and his whole house respond? According to Scripture, what is God's purpose in providing supernatural signs and wonders? (*See* John 2:11; 3:2; 7:31; 20:30, 31; Acts 8:6.)

PRACTICAL APPLICATION

> But be ye doers of the word, and not hearers only,
> deceiving your own selves.
> —James 1:22

1. After hearing this real-life story of the nobleman who sought and received healing for his son, what *encourages* you most? What *challenges* you to stretch your faith? What is your *greatest takeaway* overall?

2. Hebrews 13:8 says, "Jesus Christ [is] the same yesterday, and to day, and for ever." He performed the impossible *then*, and He is still performing the impossible *today*. Where do you need a miracle? Is it in your *health*? Your *finances*? Your *relationships*? On your *job*? Take a moment right now and write out your request and then firmly ask Him for what you need, believing He will answer you positively.

LESSON 5

TOPIC

Jesus Causes a Miraculous Catch of Fish

SCRIPTURES

1. **Luke 5:1-11** — And it came to pass, that, as the people pressed upon him to hear the word of God, he stood by the lake of Gennesaret, and saw two ships standing by the lake: but the fishermen were gone out of them, and were washing their nets. And he entered into one of

the ships, which was Simon's, and prayed him that he would thrust out a little from the land. And he sat down, and taught the people out of the ship. Now when he had left speaking, he said unto Simon, Launch out into the deep, and let down your nets for a draught. And Simon answering said unto him, Master, we have toiled all the night, and have taken nothing: nevertheless at thy word I will let down the net. And when they had this done, they enclosed a great multitude of fishes: and their net brake. And they beckoned unto their partners, which were in the other ship, that they should come and help them. And they came, and filled both the ships, so that they began to sink. When Simon Peter saw it, he fell down at Jesus' knees, saying, Depart from me; for I am a sinful man, O Lord. For he was astonished, and all that were with him, at the draught of the fishes which they had taken. And so was also James, and John, the sons of Zebedee, which were partners with Simon. And Jesus said unto Simon, Fear not; from henceforth thou shalt catch men. And when they had brought their ships to land, they forsook all, and followed him.

GREEK WORDS

1. "people" — ὄχλος (*ochlos*): a massive crowd; a mob; an enormous crowd of people

2. "pressed" — ἐπίκειμαι (*epikeimai*): to pile on top of

3. "prayed" — ἐρωτάω (*erotao*): pictures a strong request; to fervently demand with the expectation of a positive answer

4. "thrustoutalittle"—ἐπαναγαγεῖνὀλίγον(*epanagageinoligon*):anautical term meaning to put out a little into the sea

5. "launchoutinto"—ἐπανάγαγεεἰς(*epanagageeis*):anauticaltermmeaning to launch out into the sea, with the Greek word meaning into; to launch into

6. "deep" — βάθος (*bathos*): deep; depths; deep water

7. "let down" — χαλάω (*chalao*): to let down to a lower place; to go deeper

8. "nets" — δίκτυα (*diktua*): plural form of "net"

9. "draught" — ἄγρα (*agra*): a haul

10. "Master"— Ἐπιστάτα (*Epistata*): generally a master; a commander (*see* Luke 5:5); in this context, Jesus as Master and Lord

11. "toiled" — κοπιάω (*kopiao*): to work to the point of exhaustion

12. "nothing" — οὐδὲν (*ouden*): absolutely nothing at all

13. "word" — ῥῆμα (*rhema*): a thing spoken; "at Your spoken word of direction"
14. "great" — πολύς (*polus*): many; pictures a great or vast multitude
15. "multitude" — πλῆθος (*plethos*): a great number; huge amount; a bundle
16. "brake" — διαρρήσσω (*diarresso*): the tense means the nets were bursting
17. "help" — συλλαμβάνω (*sullambano*): to physically help take in the haul
18. "filled" — πλήθω (*pletho*): to fill to the maximum; fill to capacity
19. "sink" — βυθίζω (*buthidzo*): to sink; pictures a desperate situation
20. "fell down" — προσπίπτω (*prospipto*): to fall toward
21. "saying" — λέγων (*legon*): saying repetitiously
22. "sinful man" — ἁμαρτωλός (*hamartolos*): pictures a sinner; one who has missed the mark
23. "Lord" — Κύριε (*Kurie*): Lord; an absolute master or lord
24. "astonished" — θάμβος (*thambos*): dumbfounded to the point of shutting down
25. "catch" — ζωγρέω (*dzogreo*): to be actively catching; to catch alive
26. "forsook" — ἀφίημι (*aphiemi*): to permanently release; to let go; to discharge and send away with no intention of ever retrieving again
27. "followed" — ἀκολουθέω (*akoloutheo*): to follow after someone or something in a very determined and purposeful manner

SYNOPSIS

On the Sea of Galilee near the city of Capernaum, something quite amazing took place. It involved two boats, a few fishing nets, and a handful of fishermen. After speaking to a large crowd of people gathered on the shore, Jesus instructed Peter and his men to "launch out into the deep" and throw out their nets. Although the wearied men had spent all night trying to catch fish and had caught nothing, they obeyed Jesus' request, and the results were nothing short of miraculous.

The emphasis of this lesson:

In an effort to win our hearts and strengthen our faith, God will tailor-make a miracle for each person He is trying to reach. That is what Jesus did for Peter on the Sea of Galilee. He supernaturally touched and blessed Peter's business and won his heart for eternity.

Shortly after delivering the man with the unclean spirit in the synagogue, Jesus went to Peter's house and healed his mother-in-law of a lingering fever. Immediately that evening, "when the sun was setting, all they that had any sick with divers diseases brought them unto him; and he laid hands on every one of them, and healed them" (Luke 4:40). We saw in Lesson 3 that the Greek word for "healed" is *therapeuo*, which is where we get the word *therapy*. As Jesus released His *therapeutic* healing power, He required the recipients to do something to cooperate with the healing process. As they did, restorative power took root in their lives and began its work.

Jesus Made the Most of Every Teaching Moment

After leaving Peter's house the next morning, Jesus began preaching in the synagogues throughout Galilee. Eventually, He found Himself on the seashore of His new hometown of Capernaum. This brings us to another amazing miracle found in Luke chapter 5.

Verses 1 and 2 say, "And it came to pass, that, as the people pressed upon him to hear the word of God, he stood by the lake of Gennesaret, and saw two ships standing by the lake: but the fishermen were gone out of them, and were washing their nets."

In the first verse, it says the "people" pressed upon Him. The word "people" is the Greek word *ochlos*, and it describes *a massive crowd* or *a mob*. The word "pressed" is the Greek word *epikeimai*, which means *to pile on top of*. The people who had come to hear Jesus speak and receive His healing touch were literally *piling on top of Him* as He was trying to minister.

To deal with the situation, Jesus got creative. He saw two ships by the lake and "...entered into one of the ships, which was Simon's, and prayed him that he would thrust out a little from the land. And he sat down, and taught the people out of the ship" (Luke 5:3). It's important to note that Jesus will use any vehicle or vessel available to Him to bring the Word of God to as many people as possible. Peter's boat was available, so Jesus seized the opportunity.

The ship became His pulpit, and He "taught" them the Word of God. The word "taught" is the Greek word *didasko*, which as we saw in a previous lesson, refers to *a systematic form of authoritative teaching from Scripture*. Jesus was the Word made flesh (*see* John 1:14), so like a walking Bible. It was natural for Him take the Word and make it come alive everywhere He went.

Peter Submitted to the Word of the Lord

Luke 5:4 says, "Now when he had left speaking, he said unto Simon, Launch out into the deep, and let down your nets for a draught." The phrase "launch out into" is *a nautical term meaning to launch out into the sea.* And the word "draught" is the Greek word *agra*, which describes *a haul or a big catch.*

Of course, Peter could have questioned Jesus' request. After all, he was a seasoned fisherman, and Jesus was just a carpenter. But even though he thought it was a waste of time, Peter didn't argue. Instead, Peter said, "...Master, we have toiled all the night, and have taken nothing: nevertheless at thy word I will let down the net" (Luke 5:5).

Notice how Peter addressed Jesus. He called Him "Master," which is the Greek word *Epistata*, meaning *a master, a commander.* It literally means *one who stands upon the spot* or *one who is in charge.* Up until that point, Peter had had several encounters with Christ. He had seen His healing ministry, including the healing of his mother-in-law along with the healing of multitudes of people that had flooded through his house. Yet he had not repented of his sin and made Jesus the Lord of his life.

Still, Jesus wasn't discouraged with Peter. Instead, He continued to spend time with him and patiently draw him closer and closer to Himself. Peter acknowledged Him as "Master" — the One in charge — and was willing to lower the nets again even though they had "toiled" all night and caught "nothing."

The word "toiled" is the Greek word *kopiao*, which means *to work to the point of exhaustion — mental, emotional, and physical exhaustion.* This was the equivalent of Peter saying, "Lord, we don't have any strength left. We've worked all night and given it our all and have caught nothing." Interestingly, the word "nothing" means *absolutely nothing, not one thing.*

"Nevertheless," Peter added, "at Your word I will let down the net" (*see* v. 5). Essentially, Peter said, "Upon hearing your spoken word of direction, Master — the One on the spot and in charge — I will do what You have told me to do and let down the nets."

He Experienced a Miraculous, Uncontainable Catch

What was the outcome of Peter's obedience and willingness not to lean on his own natural understanding? Luke 5:6 says, "And when they had this done, they enclosed a great multitude of fishes: and their net brake." Notice they caught a "great multitude of fishes." The word "great" is the Greek word *polus*, which means *many* and pictures *a great or vast multitude*. The word "multitude" is the Greek word *plethos*, and it describes *a great number; huge amount; a bundle*. Normally, only one of these words is needed. The fact that both are used indicates the Holy Spirit is making the point that the amount of fish they caught was unbelievably huge. It was so enormous that the Scripture says "their net brake." The word "brake" is the Greek word *diarresso*, and the tense means *the nets were in the process of bursting*.

The situation became so intense, Luke 5:7 says, "And they beckoned unto their partners, which were in the other ship, that they should come and help them. And they came, and filled both the ships, so that they began to sink." The word "partners" describes *legitimate business partners*, which tells us that Peter had a major fishing enterprise.

When the partners arrived, they "filled" both ships. The Greek word for filled here is *pletho*, which means *to fill to the maximum; fill to capacity*. Interestingly, the capacity of these ships was quite large. Each vessel was ten meters long by three meters wide — thirty-two feet long by ten feet wide — and could hold the weight of five to six tons. Thus, if both these ships were filled to capacity and on the verge of sinking, Peter and his fishing partners hauled in nearly ten tons of fish.

Peter Was Brought to the Point of Surrender

This catch was simply mind-boggling. Luke 5:8 says, "When Simon Peter saw it, he fell down at Jesus' knees, saying, Depart from me; for I am a sinful man, O Lord." Peter had seen many signs and wonders Jesus did, but when the Lord miraculously touched his business, he could no longer keep his composure. The Bible says he "fell down," which is the Greek word *prospipto*, which means *to collapse*.

When Peter collapsed at Jesus' feet, he said "I'm a sinful man, O Lord." The phrase "sinful man" is the Greek word *hamartolos*, and it pictures *a sinner; one who has missed the mark*. Peter was saying, "I have really missed the mark in so many ways. I'm a sinful man, Lord."

In that moment when Peter was brought to his knees, he acknowledged Jesus as "Lord" — the Greek word *Kurie*, meaning *absolute master or lord, one with total authority*. At that moment, Peter was converted.

Luke 5:9 and 10 adds, "For he was astonished, and all that were with him, at the draught of the fishes which they had taken. And so was also James, and John, the sons of Zebedee, which were partners with Simon...." The word "astonished" is the Greek word *thambos*, which means *dumbfounded to the point of shutting down*. Peter and his partners were speechless.

Verse 10 continues, "...And Jesus said unto Simon, Fear not; from henceforth thou shalt catch men" (v.10). The Greek rendering of the word catch says, *"You will be in the process of catching men, and you're going to become professionals at it."*

Luke 5:11 tells us, "And when they had brought their ships to land, they forsook all, and followed him." The word "forsook" is a form of the Greek word *aphiemi*, which means *to permanently release; to let go; to discharge and send away with no intention of ever retrieving again*. Thus, when Peter and his associates returned to shore, they let go of their fishing enterprise and never intended to return to it. The miraculous catch of fish was a miracle designed just for him.

Also note the word "followed." It is the Greek word *akoloutheo*, and it means *to follow after someone or something in a very determined and purposeful manner*. When Peter, James, and John decided to follow Jesus, they really put their hearts into it.

STUDY QUESTIONS

Study to shew thyself approved unto God, a workman that needeth not to be ashamed, rightly dividing the word of truth.
— 2 Timothy 2:15

1. When Peter was exhausted from all his trying, he stepped out on the *word* of Jesus and received a miracle in his business. In what area do you need a miracle? Is it in your *finances*? Your *health*? Your *job*? Your *marriage*?

2. If you need verses to stand on and speak, use a Bible concordance and search by topic for what God's Word has to say on the subject. Write a few down and begin to speak them over your life and against the

enemy. Also consider the following truths about God's Word found in Hebrews 4:12, Ephesians 6:17, and Jeremiah 23:28, 29.

PRACTICAL APPLICATION

But be ye doers of the word, and not hearers only,
deceiving your own selves.
—James 1:22

1. The miraculous power and intervention of God has a way of leaving us dumbfounded. Take a moment and briefly describe the last time the Spirit of God showed up in your situation and left you speechless by what He did. How does remembering this encourage you with what you're currently facing?

2. Do you know others who are away from God who desperately need to surrender their lives to Him? What kind of tailor-made miracle do you think would really grab their heart and bring them to their knees? Begin to pray for the Holy Spirit to bring about the tailor-made miracle they need to surrender their lives to the Lordship of Jesus.

LESSON 6

TOPIC

Jesus Multiplies the Loaves and Fishes in Galilee

SCRIPTURES

1. John 6:1-13 — After these things Jesus went over the sea of Galilee, which is the sea of Tiberias. And a great multitude followed him, because they saw his miracles which he did on them that were diseased. And Jesus went up into a mountain, and there he sat with his disciples. And the passover, a feast of the Jews, was nigh. When Jesus then lifted up his eyes, and saw a great company come unto him, he saith unto Philip, Whence shall we buy bread, that these may eat? And this he said to prove him: for he himself knew what he would do. Philip answered him, Two hundred pennyworth of bread is not

sufficient for them, that every one of them may take a little. One of his disciples, Andrew, Simon Peter's brother, saith unto him, There is a lad here, which hath five barley loaves, and two small fishes: but what are they among so many? And Jesus said, Make the men sit down. Now there was much grass in the place. So the men sat down, in number about five thousand. And Jesus took the loaves; and when he had given thanks, he distributed to the disciples, and the disciples to them that were set down; and likewise of the fishes as much as they would. When they were filled, he said unto his disciples, Gather up the fragments that remain, that nothing be lost. Therefore they gathered them together, and filled twelve baskets with the fragments of the five barley loaves, which remained over and above unto them that had eaten.

GREEK WORDS

1. "great multitude"— πολὺς ὄχλος (*polus ochlos*): an enormous multitude; massive in size

2. "saw"— θεωρέω (*theoreo*): to watch act by act, like spectators watching a theatrical performance; same word for "theater"

3. "miracles"— σημεῖον (*semeion*): the verdict of a court; the signature or seal applied to documents that guaranteed their authenticity; a sign that marked key locations in a city; used in the Gospels primarily to depict miracles and supernatural events that were intended to verify and authenticate the Gospel message

4. "did"— ποιέω (*poieo*): to do; to make; to create; it is same root for the word "poet"

5. "diseased"—ἀσθενέω (*astheneo*): a word that generally describes a person frail in health; pictures those who were feeble, fragile, faint, incapacitated, disabled; can also mean to be in financial need

6. "saw"— θεάομαι (*theaomai*): this tense is from the Greek word for "theater"; to gaze upon; to fully see; to contemplate; to view; to look at intently; to fully see in full detail; to behold

7. "great company"—πολὺς ὄχλος (*polus ochlos*): massive multitude; an enormous mob of people

8. "unto"— πρὸς (*pros*): toward; directly toward

9. "prove"— πειράζω (*peiradzo*): pictures a test designed to reveal a deficiency

10. "little" — βραχύς (*brachus*): little; pictures a small amount; a fragment

11. "lad" — παιδάριον (*paidarion*): a boy; a very young boy

12. "barleyloaves"—ἄρτουςκριθίνους(*artouskrithinous*):afragileandinferior bread; a barley cracker

13. "small fishes"—ὀψάριον(*opsarion*):a small fish about the size of a sardine or minnow, usually pickled or cooked

14. "given thanks"—εὐχαριστέω(*eucharisteo*):picturesafree-flowingthankfulness; gratitude

15. "distributed" — διαδίδωμι (*diadidomi*): to divide among; to distribute among

SYNOPSIS

One of the most amazing miracles that Jesus did was multiplying the loaves and fishes to feed the thousands that had come away to hear and see Him. Today there is a church built on the traditional site where this miracle took place. Have you ever wondered how big the loaves of bread were or what the actual size of the fish were? The answers to these questions reveal the supernatural results that come from taking what you have and placing it into the hands of Jesus.

The emphasis of this lesson:

With five loaves and two fish, Jesus made a miracle dish. He fed thousands of people from a child's sack lunch, demonstrating His dynamic ability to take what seems insignificant and turn it in to something extraordinary.

A Great Multitude Followed Jesus

Jesus had performed many miracles and supernatural signs — especially in and around the city of Capernaum. With each passing day, the crowds that followed Him grew greater and greater. John 6:1 and 2 says, "After these things Jesus went over the sea of Galilee, which is the sea of Tiberias. And a great multitude followed him, because they saw his miracles which he did on them that were diseased."

Notice it says a "great multitude" followed Him. This is the Greek phrase *polus ochlos*, and it means *a multitude; enormous; massive in size*. Up until that moment, this was the largest crowd that had ever "followed" Jesus, and the Greek tense for "followed" indicates that *they kept following and fol-*

lowing and following Him. Why were they following Him so persistently? Verse 2 says, "…Because they *saw* his miracles which he did on them that were diseased."

The word "saw" here is the Greek word *theoreo*, and it means *to watch act by act, like spectators watching a theatrical performance*. It is the same word for "theater." The people who continuously followed Jesus were like spectators watching different scenes of God's power on display. They saw the "miracles" Jesus "did." The word "miracles" is the Greek word *semeion*, which describes *miraculous events*, and the word "did" is the Greek word *poieo*, which means *to do; to make;* or *to create*. It is where we get the word "poet," and it always carries the idea of *creativity or creative action*.

Jesus wasn't just doing simple miracles like healing headaches or minor illnesses. The use of the word *poieo* indicates that He had a creative flair to His healing ministry. That is, He created eyes where there were no eyes, arms where there were no arms, and feet where there were no feet. He healed those who were "diseased," which is the Greek word *astheneo*, and it generally describes *a person frail in health*. It pictures *those who were feeble, fragile, faint, incapacitated, or disabled*. The word *astheneo* can also mean *to be in financial need*. Sickness and financial depletion often go hand-in-hand. Jesus was supplying creative and supernatural solutions to unbearable situations like these.

He Saw That the People Were Hungry

Like countless other miracles, the miracle of the loaves and fishes happened near the city of Capernaum. John 6:3 and 4 says, "And Jesus went up into a mountain, and there he sat with his disciples. And the passover, a feast of the Jews, was nigh." Large crowds of people were traveling with Jesus on the Via Maris — "the way of the sea." And as they were heading to Jerusalem to celebrate the Passover, Jesus and His disciples departed from the road and found a place to sit and rest after many days of intense ministry.

John 6:5 says, "Jesus then lifted up his eyes, and saw a great company come unto him…." The word "saw" is the Greek word *theaomai*, which is also where we get the word for *theater*. It means *to gaze upon; to fully see; to contemplate; to view; to look at intently; to fully see in full detail; to behold*.

Jesus gazed intently at the people as if He were watching a dramatic presentation, and the Bible says they came "unto" Him. "Unto" is the Greek word *pros*, which means *directly toward Him*. Thousands of people were moving *directly toward* Jesus, and He was concerned for their well-being. He knew they had to be hungry after the long trip, so He "...saith unto Philip, Whence shall we buy bread, that these may eat?"

Of course, this was a silly question to ask, and Jesus knew it. They were on top of a hill in the middle of nowhere with no markets around for miles. John 6:6 says, "And this he said to prove him: for he himself knew what he would do." Jesus knew what He was about to do, but He said this to "prove" Philip. The word "prove" is the Greek word *peiradzo*, which is *a test designed to reveal a deficiency*.

Think about it. The disciples had seen with their own eyes the mighty miracles of Jesus, including the wonders of Him walking on water, turning water into wine, and casting out devils. What they had *not* seen up to this point was a miraculous multiplication of food. They had a *deficiency* in their understanding of Jesus in this area. You would think that in light of all they had seen, they would believe that Jesus would come through just as He had done so many times previously. But they didn't. Instead of rushing to faith, they rushed to doubt and began to panic.

Five Loaves and Two Fish Were All That Could Be Found

"Philip answered him, Two hundred pennyworth of bread is not suffi-cient for them, that every one of them may take a little" (John 6:7). "Two hundred pennyworth" equals 200 denarii or 200 days' worth of salary. The common wage in those days was one denarius for one day of work. Philip said, "Even if we could gather 200 days of salary in this moment and buy bread, it wouldn't be enough for everyone to have a little." The word "little" is the Greek word *brachus*, which describes *something very small; a fragment*. Two hundred denarii of bread wouldn't have given each person a fragment.

John 6:8 and 9 says, "One of his disciples, Andrew, Simon Peter's brother, saith unto him, There is a lad here, which hath five barley loaves, and two small fishes: but what are they among so many?" It's interesting to note that the word "lad" is the Greek word *paidarion*, and it describes *a very young boy, probably under the age of seven*. This boy had brought a lunch of five barley loaves and two small fishes.

Interestingly, the Greek term for "barley loaves" is *artous krithinous*, and it describes *a fragile and inferior bread; a barley cracker*. And the phrase "small fishes," is the Greek word *opsarion*, and it describes *a small fish about the size of a sardine or minnow, usually pickled or cooked.* Thus, this little boy had five barley crackers and two minnows. Why? This makes sense because he wouldn't have needed five large loaves of bread and two regular-sized fish; it would have been too much for him to eat.

There the lad stood — just about ready to reach into his pocket and pull out his little lunch that his mom had probably packed. Suddenly, one of Jesus' disciples showed up and said, "Wait! Don't eat that. Jesus needs your food." Hurriedly, the boy was rushed in front of Jesus, and he placed his five barley crackers and two minnows into His hands.

The Miracle of Multiplication

John 6:10 says, "And Jesus said, Make the men sit down. Now there was much grass in the place. So the men sat down, in number about five thousand." Interestingly, the word "men" in the Greek can describe men and women or just men. If the five thousand refers to men and women, there were 5,000 in attendance. However, if it refers to *men only* — as many scholars suggest — we would need to add to this number the wives, children, and possibly grandparents who would have been traveling to Jerusalem with them. It's estimated that as many as 40,000 people were gathered with Jesus at that time.

Yet whether it was 5,000 or 40,000, five barley crackers and two minnows weren't going to feed the crowd — regardless of how small the pieces were cut. Needless to say, the disciples saw lack in this situation, but Jesus saw opportunity — a chance to once again prove His miraculous power to His disciples and all those gathered.

Verse 11 says, "And Jesus took the loaves; and when he had given thanks, he distributed to the disciples, and the disciples to them that were set down; and likewise of the fishes as much as they would." This tells us that Jesus will take anything we place in His hands and use it for His glory. Once the crackers and minnows were in His grasp, it says He had "given thanks." This is the Greek word *eucharisteo*, which describes *a free-flowing stream of thankfulness; gratitude.*

As gratefulness was flowing, Jesus began worshiping the Father as the great Provider. In that moment, something miraculous began to happen in His hands. As He "distributed" the barley crackers and fish, which in the Greek means *to divide* or *sever*, the food multiplied in His hands! The disciples kept coming and coming, and Jesus kept giving and giving — worshiping the Father all the while.

"When they were filled, he said unto his disciples, Gather up the fragments that remain, that nothing be lost" (John 6:12). The Greek tense actually means, "When they were double filled." In other words, they ate until they were *completely filled*! The people kept eating and eating and eating until they could eat no more. Verse 13 says, "Therefore they gathered them together, and filled twelve baskets with the fragments of the five barley loaves, which remained over and above unto them that had eaten. Then those men, when they had seen the miracle that Jesus did, said, This is of a truth that prophet that should come into the world."

Can you imagine the range of emotions the disciples experienced? They went from fearful panic in the beginning to shock and utter amazement at the end, having 12 basketfuls left over. How about the little boy? He knew the minuscule amount Jesus had to work with because he had given it to Him. If he had hidden his crackers and fishes or eaten them to satisfy just his own hunger, he would have completely missed out on this amazing miracle at the hands of the Master.

STUDY QUESTIONS

Study to shew thyself approved unto God, a workman that needeth not to be ashamed, rightly dividing the word of truth.
— 2 Timothy 2:15

1. Jesus' disciples had personally observed Him do many supernatural signs, wonders, and healings. Yet when it came to the issue of not having any food for the multitudes, they immediately began to panic. Be honest. How do you react when you're confronted with a new challenge? Do you *rush to faith*, believing God will somehow come through? Or do you forget what He has done in your life and *become fearful*?

2. Clearly, God doesn't want you to worry or be anxious about anything. He wants you to trust and rest in Him. Take a few moments to meditate on Luke 12:22-31 and Romans 8:31 and 32. What is the Holy Spirit speaking to you through these passages? Also consider the proactive principles found in Proverbs 3:5, 6 and Philippians 4:6, 7.

PRACTICAL APPLICATION

**But be ye doers of the word, and not hearers only,
deceiving your own selves.
—James 1:22**

God has blessed you with many things, such as time, talent, finances, a family, and other gifts and resources. When these remain in *your* hands alone, they stay small. But when you place them in the hands of Jesus, He is able to miraculously multiply their reach and effectiveness. Stop and ask yourself these questions:

1. Is there anything in my possession that I'm withholding from God? If so, what is it?

2. What worry or fear (if any) is causing me to withhold these things?

3. How does this lesson on the loaves and fishes encourage and motivate me to entrust God with what I have?

LESSON 7

TOPIC

Jesus Heals a Centurion's Servant

SCRIPTURES

1. **Matthew 8:5-13** — And when Jesus was entered into Capernaum, there came unto him a centurion, beseeching him, and saying, Lord, my servant lieth at home sick of the palsy, grievously tormented. And Jesus saith unto him, I will come and heal him. The centurion answered and said, Lord, I am not worthy that thou shouldest come under my roof: but speak the word only, and my servant shall be healed. For I am a man under authority, having soldiers under me: and I say to this man, Go, and he goeth; and to another, Come, and he cometh; and to my servant, Do this, and he doeth it. When Jesus heard it, he marvelled, and said to them that followed, Verily I say unto you, I have not found so great faith, no, not in Israel. And I say unto you, That many shall come from the east and west, and shall sit down with Abraham, and Isaac, and Jacob, in the kingdom of heaven.

But the children of the kingdom shall be cast out into outer darkness: there shall be weeping and gnashing of teeth. And Jesus said unto the centurion, Go thy way; and as thou hast believed, so be it done unto thee. And his servant was healed in the selfsame hour.

GREEK WORDS

1. "centurion"—ἑκατοντάρχης (*hekatontarches*): a captain over 100 hundred men; a centurion in the Roman army

2. "beseeching"—παρακαλέω (*parakaleo*): to plead with someone by appealing to them; the tense means continually beseeching

3. "saying"— λέγων (*legon*): saying repetitiously

4. "servant"— παῖς (*pais*): a small child; a little boy

5. "Lord" (vv. 6, 8) — Κύριε (*Kurie*): Lord; an absolute master or lord

6. "lieth"—βέβληται (*bebletai*): a form of βάλλω (*ballo*): to throw; in context, thrown down, hurled down, unable to get up, perhaps even critically ill

7. "sick of the palsy"—παραλυτικός (*paralutikos*): crippled; paralyzed; as a result, bedfast

8. "grievously"— δεινῶς (*deinos*): terribly; horribly; from the word δειλός, which notably depicts fear

9. "tormented"—βασανίζω (*basanidzo*): to torment or torture; the form used in this verse denotes unending torment and torture

10. "heal"— θεραπεύω (*therapeuo*): therapy; a healing touch that requires corresponding actions

11. "healed"— ἰάομαι (*iaomai*): to cure; to doctor; pictures a healing power that progressively reverses a condition; mostly denoted healing that came to pass over a period of time; for this reason, the word is often translated as a "treatment," "cure," or "remedy"; depicts one who is progressively healed rather than instantaneously healed

12. "marvelled"—θαυμάζω (*thaumadzo*): to wonder; to be at a loss of words; to be shocked and amazed; to be bewildered

13. "found"— εὑρίσκω (*heurisko*): to find or to discover; pictures a moment when one makes a surprising discovery; usually points to a discovery made due to an intense investigation, scientific study, or scholarly research

14. "cast out" — ἐκβάλλω (*ekballo*): to forcibly evict; to throw out; to cast out; to expel; to drive out; to kick out; to cast out; historically used to describe a nation that forcibly removed lawbreakers from its borders

15. "go" — ὕπαγε (*hupage*): literally, to go under

SYNOPSIS

Capernaum was known as the "city of Jesus." Once word got out about Jesus' supernatural power, people began swarming into Capernaum from all across the region to receive His healing touch and hear Him teach God's Word. Peter's home is where Christ stayed, and it became His base of operation throughout His ministry. Indeed, the people in and around Capernaum witnessed more signs, wonders, and healings than the people of any other city in Israel. One of these miracles was the healing of the centurion's servant.

The emphasis of this lesson:

Jesus miraculously healed the child of a centurion who lived in Capernaum, and He did it without laying a hand on him. He simply spoke the word, and the centurion believed and received the healing for his son. No one in all Israel had exhibited such great faith.

The Centurion Was Stationed in Capernaum

As we discovered in our first lesson, Capernaum was a very affluent and influential border town. It was located on the Via Maris, which was the main highway that ran from Damascus in the north to Egypt in the south. This international community had many tourists and travelers passing through, and as they entered the city, they were required to pay taxes. Thus, there was a tax-collection office there — the same office where Matthew worked and where Jesus found him when He called him into ministry.

As a result of Capernaum's international status and high level of wealth, there was also a strong military presence in the city. Many soldiers were stationed there for protection, including one particular centurion. His story begins in Matthew chapter 8: "When Jesus was entered into Capernaum, there came unto him a centurion, beseeching him, and saying, Lord, my servant lieth at home sick of the palsy, grievously tormented" (vv. 5, 6).

First, notice the word "beseeching." It is the Greek word *parakaleo*, which is a compound of two words: the word *para*, meaning *to come alongside*, and the word *kaleo*, meaning *to call out*. When these two words are put together to form *parakaleo*, it means *to plead with someone by appealing to them*. The tense here indicates something continual and ongoing.

This powerful centurion — a captain or commander of 100 soldiers — came right alongside Jesus and began to call out and plead with Him to come and heal his servant. This must have been shocking for the people of Capernaum to see — a military man of high status and great clout, coming alongside Jesus and pleading with Him to answer his request.

The word "saying" in verse 6 is the Greek word *legon*, which means *to repetitiously say*. Verse 6 would better be translated, "He kept saying and saying and saying." This highly dignified officer was spilling his heart out to Jesus. His servant was in trouble, and he was willing to do whatever it took to see him get better.

Also note how the centurion addressed Jesus. Verse 6 says he called Him "Lord," which is the Greek word *Kurie*, a form of the word *Kurios*, and it means *absolute master or lord*. The centurion recognized Jesus as Master and Lord over him and his situation, which is exactly what we need to do in every situation we face.

It Was His *Son*, Not His Servant, Who Was Sick

It is very interesting to note that in the *King James Version* of Matthew 8:6, it says that the military commander told Jesus, "…my servant lieth at home sick of the palsy, grievously tormented." The word "servant" is the Greek term *pais*, which actually means *a small child; a little boy*. A literal translation would be, "My *small child* lieth at home sick.…"

This is significant because Roman soldiers were not permitted to be married. When a man enlisted in the Roman army, he was committed to service for 25 years and could not marry until his time was completed. When soldiers were dispatched, they were gone for a very long time. If they had been allowed to marry, they would have been greatly distracted on the battlefield by thoughts of their wife and family back home, which could have proven disastrous.

Another reason soldiers were not allowed to marry was the motivation it created. If a soldier died on the battlefield, he had no children to carry on his lineage. Therefore, he would fight much harder in battle to survive and finish his 25-year commitment so he could return home to marry and raise a family.

Thus, the centurion who sought out Jesus was not married according to Roman law. The fact that he had a small child (*pais*) and he wasn't married meant his child was illegitimate. He obviously had an immoral relationship with someone. Yet when he came to Jesus for help, Jesus never rebuked him for it. He never said, "What do you mean, asking Me to heal your illegitimate child… You've been involved in a sinful, immoral relationship." On the contrary, Jesus listened and was willing to help.

Understanding the Severity of the Child's Condition

Looking again at Matthew 8:6, the centurion said, "…Lord, my servant lieth at home sick of the palsy, grievously tormented." The word "lieth" is a form of the Greek word *ballo*, which means *to throw*. In context, it means *thrown down, hurled down, unable to get up, perhaps even critically ill*. In other words, the centurion's son had been thrown into bed and was unable to get up.

He also said his child was "sick of the palsy," which in Greek is the word *paralutikos*, and it means *to be crippled or paralyzed*. The child had lost his ability to function. Something had happened to his muscles, his nerves, or his sinews that left him paralyzed, and as a result, he was "grievously tormented." The word "grievously" is the Greek word *deinos*, which means *to be terribly*, or in this case, *horribly*, tormented. It is a derivative of the word *deilos*, which notably depicts *fear*.

When a person is sick, they are often also plagued with fear. Many times they are afraid that they will never feel normal again or that they will never again live a normal life. This type of fear is "grievous" — it is a *horrible, terrible* "torment."

The word "tormented" is the Greek word *basanidzo*, which means *to torment or torture*. The form used in this verse denotes *unending torment and torture*. The word *basanidzo* is the word commonly used in the gospels to describe people who are grievously vexed by demon spirits.

How Did Jesus Respond?

Matthew 8:7 says, "And Jesus saith unto him, I will come and heal him." Jesus heard that this child was thrown into bed; he was sick, paralyzed, and grievously tormented by fear. Moved with compassion, Jesus immediately said, "I will come and heal him."

The word "heal" is the Greek word *therapeuo*, which is the term most frequently used in the gospels to describe the healing ministry of Jesus. It is *a healing touch that requires corresponding actions*, and it is where we get the word "therapy."

When Jesus healed a person with a withered hand, He required him to stretch out his hand. If someone was lame and lying on a mat, Jesus would require him to pick up his mat and walk. In the same way a physical therapist requires patients to cooperate with the recovery process, Jesus required those who received healing to cooperate with the power of God.

The Centurion's Faith Was Unprecedented

When Jesus said that He was willing to go and heal the boy, "the centurion answered and said, Lord, I am not worthy that thou shouldest come under my roof: but speak the word only, and my servant shall be healed. For I am a man under authority, having soldiers under me: and I say to this man, Go, and he goeth; and to another, Come, and he cometh; and to my servant, Do this, and he doeth it" (Matthew 8:8, 9).

Notice the word "healed." It is the Greek word *iaomai*, and it pictures *a healing power that progressively reverses a condition*. It mostly denoted *healing that came to pass over a period of time*. For this reason, the word is often translated as a "treatment," "cure," or "remedy." It depicts *one who is progressively healed rather than instantaneously healed*. The use of this word reveals the centurion's level of faith. He wasn't asking for an instantaneous miracle; he was believing for a progressive healing once Jesus spoke the Word.

What is also interesting about the centurion's faith was his understanding of authority. He told Jesus, "You don't need to come to my house. Just speak the word of healing, and I know it will happen." Matthew 8:10 says, "When Jesus heard it, he marvelled, and said to them that followed, Verily I say unto you, I have not found so great faith, no, not in Israel."

The word "marvelled" is the Greek word *thaumadzo*, which means *to wonder; to be at a loss of words; to be shocked and amazed; to be bewildered*. Jesus was absolutely stunned at the centurion's level of faith. He said He had not "found" anyone with such great faith out of all the people in Israel.

The word "found" in the Greek is the word *heurisko*, which means *to find or to discover*. It pictures a moment when one *makes a surprising discovery, usually as a result of an intense investigation, scientific study, or scholarly research*. This tells us that Jesus had been studying and looking for a high-quality faith among the Jews, but He didn't find it. Instead, He found it among the Gentiles — in a pagan Roman soldier.

The Significance of Jesus' Statement About Outer Darkness

As Jesus marveled at the faith of the centurion, He said, "…Many shall come from the east and west, and shall sit down with Abraham, and Isaac, and Jacob, in the kingdom of heaven. But the children of the kingdom shall be cast out into outer darkness: there shall be weeping and gnashing of teeth" (Matthew 8:12).

To understand Jesus' statement, we need to examine a practice in the ancient world that is mostly unfamiliar. In that day, large cities had very tall protective walls, and often they would dump their garbage and unused food over the top of those walls. During the night, when it was dark, the lions outside of the city would come and pillage through the garbage looking for something to eat.

Why is this important? Well, the presence of the lions outside the city was used to help determine whether or not a person was truly innocent. In those days, if a person was tried but could not be proven guilty of a crime it was believed he committed, the city authorities would tie him up and place him outside the city walls for the entire night. They called this "outer darkness." The officials believed that if someone survived the lions and was alive the next morning, he was not guilty.

However, there was a problem. When they went out to find the suspect the next morning, even if he survived the lions, his teeth were totally ground away. This was the result of being totally stricken with fear at the presence of the prowling lions. These people were put into outer darkness — a place of torment where they literally had weeping and gnashing of teeth.

By using this phrase, Jesus was saying, "There's going to be a lot of weeping and gnashing of teeth when people realize what they could have had but missed out on because they would not believe. This includes people in Israel, people in the Kingdom, and people who should have known how to use their faith but didn't. They may get through life, but they're going to miss so much because they never really used their faith." That's really what Jesus was teaching here.

What You Believe Is What Will Be Done

Matthew 8:13 goes on to say, "And Jesus said unto the centurion, Go thy way; and as thou hast believed, so be it done unto thee. And his servant was healed in the selfsame hour." The word "go" here is the Greek word *hupage*, and it literally means *to go under authority*.

Essentially, Jesus said, "I have spoken the word of healing, and your son is taken care of. You have come under My authority, and now I'm sending you away under the power of My word. Go! The healing is released exactly as you have believed." The centurion left, and when he returned home he discovered that his small child had been healed at the exact same time Jesus had spoken it.

Like the centurion, you must believe and embrace the words of Jesus. Accept and respond to what He has said in His Word and what His Spirit speaks to you in your heart. What you believe and act on is what will take place.

STUDY QUESTIONS

Study to shew thyself approved unto God, a workman that needeth not to be ashamed, rightly dividing the word of truth.
— 2 Timothy 2:15

1. After hearing the account of the miraculous healing of the centurion's servant, what new insights did you learn? What aspects of Jesus' character had you not seen before now?
2. Even though the centurion had been in an immoral relationship, Jesus did not judge or rebuke him. Instead, He willingly answered his request. What does this say to you about His desire and willingness to help you in spite of your past mistakes? Consider Jesus' words in John 3:16-18.

PRACTICAL APPLICATION

But be ye doers of the word, and not hearers only, deceiving your own selves.
— James 1:22

1. Like the centurion, do you have a child or loved one who is in trouble? Is he or she sick or away from God? How does this true story encourage you to "beseech" Jesus for a miracle in his or her life?

2. The Bible says the centurion took Jesus at His word and believed that his child was healed. How about you? What are you believing about God's goodness, His wisdom, and His power regarding your situation? Is your belief in line with His Word?

LESSON 8

TOPIC

Jesus Heals a Paralyzed Man Who Came Through the Roof

SCRIPTURES

1. **Mark 2:1-12** — And again he entered into Capernaum after some days; and it was noised that he was in the house. And straightway many were gathered together, insomuch that there was no room to receive them, no, not so much as about the door: and he preached the word unto them. And they come unto him, bringing one sick of the palsy, which was borne of four. And when they could not come nigh unto him for the press, they uncovered the roof where he was: and when they had broken it up, they let down the bed wherein the sick of the palsy lay. When Jesus saw their faith, he said unto the sick of the palsy, Son, thy sins be forgiven thee. But there were certain of the scribes sitting there, and reasoning in their hearts. Why doth this man thus speak blasphemies? who can forgive sins but God only? And immediately when Jesus perceived in his spirit that they so reasoned within themselves, he said unto them, Why reason ye these things in your hearts? Whether is it easier to say to the sick of the palsy, Thy sins be forgiven thee; or to say, Arise, and take up thy bed, and walk? But that ye may know that the Son of man hath power on earth to forgive sins, (he saith to the sick of the palsy,) I say unto thee, Arise, and take up thy bed, and go thy way into thine house. And immediately he arose, took up the bed, and went forth before them

all; insomuch that they were all amazed, and glorified God, saying, We never saw it on this fashion.

GREEK WORDS

1. "many" — πολλοί (*polloi*): a great quantity; something that is huge numerically

2. "no room"—μηκέτιχωρεῖν (*meketichorein*):no more space;no more room for receiving or holding something

3. "preached" — ἐλάλει (*elalei*): to be speaking or talking

4. "the word"—τὸν λόγον (*ton logon*):with a definite article,it is a reference to the Word of God

5. "bringing" — φέρω (*phero*): to physically carry

6. "sick of the palsy"—παραλυτικός (*paralutikos*): pictures one who suffers the effects of a stroke; paralyzed

7. "[could not] come nigh unto"—προσφέρω (*prosphero*):in context,pictures an inability to draw physically near [to Jesus]

8. "press" — ὄχλος (*ochlus*): a crowd, a mob, or a multitude

9. "uncovered" — ἀποστεγάζω (*apostegadzo*): to remove a roof

10. "broken up"—ἐξορύσσω (*exorusso*):to pluck out the eyes;to gouge out;to dig out; to dig through; to extract and remove

11. "let down" — χαλάω (*chalao*): to let down from a higher place to a lower place

12. "bed" — κράβαττος (*krabattos*): a bed, pallet, or mattress for the poor

13. "saw" — ὁράω (*horao*): to behold; to delightfully view

14. "forgiven" — ἀφίημι (*aphiemi*): to forgive; to permanently dismiss; to release; to let go; to irretrievably remove

15. "blasphemies"—βλασφημέω (*blasphemeo*):pictures profane,foul,unclean language; language that is offensive (Mark 2:7)

16. "perceived"—ἐπιγινώσκω (*epiginosko*):to know;to know a subject inside and out; to know from top to bottom; pictures a thorough and complete knowledge; first-hand knowledge

17. "easier" — εὐκοπώτερον (*eukopoteron*): to do with nearly no effort; to accomplish effortlessly (Mark 2:9)

18. "go thy way" — ὑπάγω (*hupago*): to go away under someone's authority

19. "immediately" — εὐθὺς (*euthus*): in that very instant; immediately

20. "before"—ἔμπροσθεν (*emprosthen*): in the presence of; before the face; in the eyesight of; publicly

21. "amazed"— ἐξίστημι (*existemi*): to be knocked out of one's wits; to be "beside oneself"; astonished, flabbergasted, overwhelmed, stupefied; to be speechless or at a total loss for words

SYNOPSIS

As we have seen in previous lessons, Peter lived in the city of Capernaum, and when Jesus was there, He stayed at Peter's home. The ancient ruins of this site were noted by historians as early as the Fourth Century. The walls were still standing and the edifice had been converted in to a church, and it can still be seen today. It was in this house that Jesus performed countless miracles, including the healing of a paralyzed man who was brought to Jesus by his four friends.

The emphasis of this lesson:

Four men carried their paralyzed friend to Jesus to be healed. Motivated by faith, they let nothing stand in their way — neither the crowds of people, nor the roof of Peter's house. When Jesus saw their great faith, He miraculously healed the man and sent him on his way.

Jesus Was Preaching the Word at Peter's House

Mark 2:1 says, "And again he [Jesus] entered into Capernaum after some days; and it was noised that he was in the house." The news of Jesus arrival was "noised" all around the region. This word "noised" in the Greek refers to *a big ruckus*. In other words, everyone was talking about the fact that Jesus was in town. Specifically, He was in "the house," which refers to Peter's house.

Verse 2 says, "And straightway many were gathered together, insomuch that there was no room to receive them, no, not so much as about the door: and he preached the word unto them." The word "straightway" in Greek means *immediately; without delay*. The moment people heard Jesus was at Peter's house, "many" gathered to see Him. This word "many" is the Greek word *polloi*, and it describes *a great quantity; something that is huge numerically*. The crowd that gathered was so large, there was "no room" to fit everyone. The phrase "no room" indicates there was *no more space; no more room for receiving or holding something*.

Seizing the opportunity, Jesus "preached the word." The Greek word for "preached" is *elalei*, which describes *speaking or talking*, and "the word" refers specifically to *the Word of God*. The use of a definite article here confirms this. Jesus didn't yell or scream the Word at them; He simply began conversing with them from His heart about the Scriptures. As He preached the Word, the Holy Spirit confirmed the Word with signs and wonders.

A Paralyzed Man Was Placed Before Him

"And they come unto him, bringing one sick of the palsy, which was borne of four" (Mark 2:3). The word "bringing" is the Greek word *phero*, which means *to physically carry*. This man was physically carried to Jesus being "sick of the palsy." The phrase "sick of the palsy" is the Greek word *paralutikos*, and it pictures *one who suffers the effects of a stroke or is paralyzed*.

The fact that this man was carried by four men implies that he was heavy. Normally, two could have handled such a task, but if he was a larger, heavier man, he would require more help. People who are paralyzed and bedridden don't usually exercise, so they tend to gain weight from their sedentary condition, as this man did.

Mark 2:4 says, "And when they could not come nigh unto him for the press, they uncovered the roof where he was: and when they had broken it up, they let down the bed wherein the sick of the palsy lay." There are several things to note in this passage, starting with the phrase "could not come nigh unto." This is the Greek word *prosphero*, and in context, it pictures *an inability to draw physically near to Jesus*.

Next, is the word "press" — the Greek word *ochlus* — and it describes *a crowd, a mob, or a multitude*. The mob of people that had filled Peter's house was so great that the friends of the paralyzed man could not get him through the door to see Jesus. To overcome this challenge, "they uncovered the roof where he was." The word "uncovered" in the Greek literally means *they removed the roof*.

The Scripture goes on to say, "…and when they had broken it up, they let down the bed wherein the sick of the palsy lay." This phrase "broken it up" tells us how they removed the roof. It is the Greek word *exorusso*, and it describes a very violent act. It means *to pluck out the eyes; to gouge out; to dig out; to dig through; to extract and remove*.

The four friends of the paralytic were so desperate to get him in front of Jesus that they dug through the clay and straw roof and made a hole large enough to let him down while he was still on his bed. The word "bed" is the Greek word *krabattos*, and it describes *a bed, pallet, or mattress for the poor.* It was the place on which this sick man had been fixated and was living his life.

Jesus Saw and Was Moved by Their Faith

Mark 2:5 says, "When Jesus saw their faith, he said unto the sick of the palsy, Son, thy sins be forgiven thee." The word "saw" is the Greek word *horao*, which means *to behold* or *to delightfully view.* How did Jesus see their faith? He saw it in their actions. They believed so strongly that Jesus could heal their paralyzed friend that they gouged a hole in the roof and lowered their friend down in front of Him.

The intensity of their faith impressed Jesus and moved Him to say, "Son, thy sins be forgiven thee." The word "forgiven" is from the Greek word *aphiemi*, which means *to permanently dismiss; to release; to let go; to irretrievably remove.* Jesus permanently dismissed and removed the sick man's sins, never to retrieve them again.

"But there were certain of the scribes sitting there, and reasoning in their hearts. Why doth this man thus speak blasphemies? who can forgive sins but God only?" (Mark 2:6, 7). The word "blasphemies" here specifically refers to *religiously foul language.* The religious leaders were thinking to themselves, *How dare He say He has the power to forgive! Only God can forgive sins!*

Verse 8 says, "And immediately when Jesus perceived in his spirit that they so reasoned within themselves, he said unto them, Why reason ye these things in your hearts?" The word "perceived" is the Greek word *epiginosko*, which means *to know a subject inside and out; to know from top to bottom; it pictures a thorough and complete knowledge; firsthand knowledge.* The thoughts of the religious leaders were not hidden from Jesus; He was totally aware of them, just as He is totally aware of our thoughts as well.

Jesus Demonstrated His Power and Authority To Heal and Forgive Sins

Mindful of what they were thinking, Jesus turned to them and said, "Whether is it easier to say to the sick of the palsy, Thy sins be forgiven thee; or to say, Arise, and take up thy bed, and walk?" (Mark 2:9). The

Greek word for "easier" is *eukopoteron,* and it means *to do something with nearly no effort; to accomplish effortlessly.* Thus, Jesus said, "It requires virtually no effort for Me to forgive someone's sin or to heal someone who is paralyzed. I have the power and authority and am well able to do both."

Jesus went on to say, "But that ye may know that the Son of man hath power on earth to forgive sins, (he saith to the sick of the palsy,) I say unto thee, Arise, and take up thy bed, and go thy way into thine house" (Mark 2:10, 11). The phrase "go thy way" is the Greek word *hupago* — a word that regularly appears with the telling of Jesus' miracles. It means *to go away under someone's authority.* Essentially, Jesus said, "I release you from your physical sickness; now go under the power and authority of My word."

After Jesus uttered these words, Mark 2:12 says, "Immediately he arose, took up the bed, and went forth before them all; insomuch that they were all amazed, and glorified God, saying, We never saw it on this fashion." The word "immediately" is the Greek word *euthus,* which means *in that very instant; immediately.* And the word "before" is the Greek word *emprosthen,* meaning *in the presence of; before the face; in the eyesight of; publicly.* When Jesus spoke the word of healing, instantly the paralyzed man was made whole before their very eyes and began to walk.

Scripture says that those who witnessed this miracle were "amazed," which is the Greek word *existemi,* and it means *to be knocked out of one's wits; to be "besides oneself"; to be astonished, flabbergasted, overwhelmed, stupefied, speechless, or at a total loss for words.* The people had never seen anything like this and didn't know how to respond. All they could do was turn to one another and keep saying again and again, "We have never seen anything like this."

STUDY QUESTIONS

**Study to shew thyself approved unto God, a workman that needeth
not to be ashamed, rightly dividing the word of truth.
— 2 Timothy 2:15**

1. When Jesus saw the four men dig through the roof to get their sick friend in front of Him, He was delighted by their faith. Take a moment to read James 2:14-26. What is the Holy Spirit speaking to you in this passage about the connection between your faith and your actions?

2. Just as the religious leaders' thoughts were not hidden from Jesus, neither are your thoughts hidden from Him. Carefully read Hebrews 4:13 and Romans 14:10-12. What is the Holy Spirit speaking to you in these verses? (*See* Matthew 10:26; 1 John 3:20.)

PRACTICAL APPLICATION

> But be ye doers of the word, and not hearers only,
> deceiving your own selves.
> —James 1:22

1. The four friends of the paralytic man had strong faith and did everything they could do to get their friend to Jesus. Be honest. How badly do you want God to move in your life? What evidence confirms your answer?

2. Do you have a friend who desperately needs to be healed but can't get to Jesus on his or her own? Who is it? What kind of healing does this person need? In what ways can Jesus see your faith for this individual in action?

3. Jesus gave the paralyzed man His word of authority that he was healed. In obedience, the man acted on it and received his healing. What specific word of authority has the Lord given you regarding your situation? Have you obediently acted on it? If not, what is keeping you from doing so?

LESSON 9

TOPIC

Jesus Calms a Storm on the Sea of Galilee

SCRIPTURES

1. Mark 4:35-41 — And the same day, when the even was come, he saith unto them, Let us pass over unto the other side. And when they had sent away the multitude, they took him even as he was in the ship. And there were also with him other little ships. And there arose

a great storm of wind, and the waves beat into the ship, so that it was now full. And he was in the hinder part of the ship, asleep on a pillow: and they awake him, and say unto him, Master, carest thou not that we perish? And he arose, and rebuked the wind, and said unto the sea, Peace, be still. And the wind ceased, and there was a great calm. And he said unto them, Why are ye so fearful? how is it that ye have no faith? And they feared exceedingly, and said one to another, What manner of man is this, that even the wind and the sea obey him?

2. Ephesians 6:12 — For we wrestle not against flesh and blood, but against principalities, against powers, against the rulers of the darkness of this world, against spiritual wickedness in high places.

GREEK WORDS

1. "there arose" — γίνομαι (*ginomai*): to take by surprise; to take off guard; pictures something not anticipated

2. "storm" — λαῖλαψ (*lailaps*): atmospheric turbulence

3. "waves" — κύματα (*kumata*): billowing waves; one wave after another; a succession of waves (*see* Mark 4:37)

4. "beat into" — ἐπιβάλλω (*epiballo*): to pick up and throw; to throw over; to throw against

5. "awake" — ἐγείρω (*egeiro*): to rouse; to rise; to awake; to resurrect

6. "perish" — ἀπόλλυμι (*apollumi*): to undo; to perish; to come to pieces

7. "rebuke" — ἐπιτιμάω (*epitimao*): in context, to speak dishonorably to someone; to sternly speak against; to chide; to rebuke

8. "peace be still" — φιμόω (*phimoo*): to muzzle; to silence; to still

9. "obey" — ὑπακούω (*hupakouo*): to submit and explicitly obey; to fall in line when an order is given

SYNOPSIS

Another day of ministry in the city of Capernaum had just come to a close. "And the same day, when the even was come, he [Jesus] saith unto them, Let us pass over unto the other side. And when they had sent away the multitude, they took him even as he was in the ship. And there were also with him other little ships" (Mark 4:35, 36). On the other side of the Sea of Galilee was the country of the Gadarenes, and Jesus had important work to do there.

Mark 5 later tells us that in that region there lived a man possessed with a legion of demons. The entire countryside was terrorized and held captive in fear by the evil forces working through him (*see also* Matthew 8:28). As Jesus and His disciples were heading to the area to deliver the demoniac from the devil's grip, the enemy attacked, stirring up a storm of hurricane proportions.

The emphasis of this lesson:

Just as Jesus had power and authority over the wind and the waves on the Sea of Galilee, He has power and authority over all the storms that arise in your life. If you will call out to Him, He will hear and answer you, delivering you from the devil's devious attacks.

A Great Storm Arose

Mark 4:37 says, "And there arose a great storm of wind, and the waves beat into the ship, so that it was now full." Notice the phrase "there arose." It is the Greek word *ginomai*, and it means *to take by surprise; to take off guard; it pictures something not anticipated*. This verse could be translated, "And suddenly, out of nowhere, there arose a great storm of wind that took us completely off guard; it was totally unexpected, and we had no idea from where it came."

Keep in mind that many of Jesus' disciples were seasoned fishermen. They knew the waterways and the weather patterns of the region very well. If a natural storm had been brewing that night, they would certainly have recognized the warning signs and never gone out in their boat. However, when they started out, the skies were clear and the water was calm.

The Bible says that as they were en route to their destination, a "great" storm of wind arose. The word "great" is the Greek word *megas*, which indicates *something enormous*. This enormous "storm" was not a rainstorm; it was an enormous "storm" of wind. The word "storm" in the Greek is *lailaps*, and it describes *atmospheric turbulence*. Although the effects of the turbulence could be felt, the source of the turbulent force could not be seen.

The Source of the Invisible Force

A closer look at Mark 4:37 reveals that there was nothing natural about the storm that arose. It says, "…And the waves beat into the ship, so that it was now full." The word "waves" is the Greek word *kumata*, and it describes *billowing waves; one wave after another; a succession of waves.* As one monstrous wave after another slammed against the ship, it was clear that Jesus and His disciples had become the target of a demonic assault.

Scripture says the waves "beat into" the ship. The words "beat into" are from the Greek word *epiballo*. It is the compound of two words: *epi*, meaning *over*, and *ballo*, meaning *to throw*. When the two words are put together to form the word *epiballo*, it means *to throw over* or *to throw toward*. This word is never used to describe the actions of nature. Rather, it is always used to describe the actions of a person or entity.

By using the word *epiballo*, the Holy Spirit informs us that this was the work of an invisible entity. An unseen force was piling up water and throwing it toward the boat again and again. This was Satan's attempt to sink the ship and drown Jesus and His disciples. The devil knew that if Jesus reached the other side, he was going to lose control of the demoniac of Gadara as well as his influence in the entire region. So he fought fiercely against the Lord and His disciples.

Where Was Jesus?

Scripture says that Jesus "…was in the hinder part of the ship, asleep on a pillow…" (Mark 4:38). While the storm was raging, Jesus was sleeping on a "pillow." This word "pillow" in the Greek describes a cushion that fit snugly in the corner of the ship. This was where Jesus was sleeping. He was nestled in the peace of God, not worried one bit about making it to the other side. He knew that God had told Him to cross over to the country of the Gadarenes, and nothing could keep Him from getting where God had called Him to be.

Meanwhile, as the storm continued, the disciples began to panic greatly, and the Bible says, "…They awake him." The word "awake" in Greek is *egeiro*, which means *to rouse; to rise; to awake; to resurrect*. Thus, the disciples *resurrected* Jesus from His sleep. They jerked Him off His pillow and said, "…Master, carest thou not that we perish?" The word "master" is the Greek word *epistata*, and it means *the one on the spot who is totally in charge*. They were asking Jesus to get up and exercise His supernatural authority and power over their situation.

Interestingly, the original Greek structure of the phrase "carest thou not that we perish" actually says, "Is there no care in You toward us that we are perishing?" The word "perish" is from the Greek word *apollumi*, which means *to undo or unravel; to perish; to come to pieces* or *come apart at the seams.* This describes how the disciples were feeling — they felt like they were coming apart at the seams in the midst of the raging storm.

How Did Jesus Respond to the Disciples' Plea?

Mark 4:39 says, "And he arose, and rebuked the wind, and said unto the sea, Peace, be still. And the wind ceased, and there was a great calm." The moment the disciples called to Jesus for help, He responded. You can expect Him to respond to you, too, when you call on Him for help.

The Bible says Jesus "rebuked" the wind. The Greek word for "rebuked" is *epitimao,* and it means *to speak dishonorably to someone; to sternly speak against; to chide; to rebuke.* It is the same word that was used in judicial courts when the judgment against a criminal was being verbalized and enacted.

This tells us that when Jesus "rebuked" the wind, He didn't stand up and say, "I rebuke you, wind!" On the contrary, He stood up and began to verbally assassinate the wind. That is, He had a conversation with the unseen spiritual force behind the storm, and with His words He assaulted, belittled, demeaned, and humiliated it.

Once Jesus was finished rebuking the invisible power causing the storm, He said to the sea, "Peace, be still." Although this phrase is difficult to translate, "peace, be still" in effect means *to muzzle; to silence;* or *to still.* Actually, the very best way to explain it is to say that Jesus muzzled the sea, telling it to *"shhh."*

Jesus Addressed the *Source,* Not the Symptoms

It is important to note that the disciples thought their problem was the waves. Thus, that is what they focused on and fought against throughout the night. Again and again, they bailed water and wrangled with the waves. Nevertheless, by only dealing with the *symptoms* of the problem and not the source, the situation stayed the same.

Jesus, on the other hand, looked beyond the symptoms and addressed the source — the unseen evil entity in the atmosphere. He knew that they didn't have a "wave" problem; they had a *spiritual* problem. And spiritual problems can only be solved with spiritual solutions. That is why Jesus "rebuked" the demonic force that was stirring up the wind and propelling the waves. He verbally assaulted the enemy with the words of His mouth, humiliating and demeaning it.

When He did, the Bible says, "The wind ceased, and there was a great calm" (Mark 4:39). Although the evening began with a great *storm*, it ended with a great *calm*. This lets us know that whatever the devil tries to do, Jesus will match it and defeat it. If you have had a great sickness, there is going to be a great healing. If you have had great financial lack, there is going to be great financial blessing.

Once the great calm arrived, Jesus turned to His disciples and said to them, "...Why are ye so fearful? how is it that ye have no faith?" (Mark 4:40). He was saying, "Hey guys, why did you wake Me up? You could have spoken to the invisible realm and dealt with this yourselves. You really didn't need Me. Where is your faith?"

Verse 41 goes on to say, "And they feared exceedingly, and said one to another, What manner of man is this, that even the wind and the sea obey him?" The word "obey" here is a military term, and it means *to submit and explicitly obey; to fall in line when an order is given.* When Jesus lifted His voice and rebuked the enemy, the wind and the waves *fell in line* as they were told. The natural realm was filled with peace once the spiritual realm had been dealt with.

Remember, "we wrestle not against flesh and blood, but against principalities, against powers, against the rulers of the darkness of this world, against spiritual wickedness in high places" (Ephesians 6:12). If you will lift your voice when the enemy attacks, Jesus will speak through you and rebuke him.

STUDY QUESTIONS

> Study to shew thyself approved unto God, a workman that needeth
> not to be ashamed, rightly dividing the word of truth.
> — 2 Timothy 2:15

1. According to Acts 2:21 and Psalm 34:4, 15-20, when you call on the Lord for help, what can you expect to happen? Also consider Romans 10:13; Joel 2:32; Psalm 94:9; First Peter 3:12; and Second Samuel 22:7.
2. God's Word tells us what we're to do to stand against the enemy. Take a few minutes to meditate on First Peter 5:6-9 and Ephesians 6:10-18.

What is the Holy Spirit showing you in these passages about standing against the unseen forces of evil?

PRACTICAL APPLICATION

> **But be ye doers of the word, and not hearers only,**
> **deceiving your own selves.**
> **— James 1:22**

1. When you suddenly find yourself in the midst of an unexpected storm, what does it usually indicate is just ahead in your life? How does this encourage you?

2. If you focus on and fight against the *symptoms* of your problems like the disciples did, what will happen to you? What will likely happen concerning your situation?

3. Where in your life is there a storm raging right now? Is it in your *relationships*? Your *health*? Your *finances*? At your *job*? Briefly describe the situation.

4. If the devil is trying to stop you from getting to where God wants you to be, take time now to pray and call on the Lord for help.

LESSON 10

TOPIC

Jesus Casts a Legion of Demons Out of a Demoniac

SCRIPTURES

1. **Mark 5:1-20** — And they came over unto the other side of the sea, into the country of the Gadarenes. And when he was come out of the ship, immediately there met him out of the tombs a man with an unclean spirit, who had his dwelling among the tombs; and no man could bind him, no, not with chains: because that he had been often bound with fetters and chains, and the chains had been plucked asunder by him, and the fetters broken in pieces: neither could any man tame him. And always, night and day, he was in the moun-

tains, and in the tombs, crying, and cutting himself with stones. But when he saw Jesus afar off, he ran and worshipped him, and cried with a loud voice, and said, What have I to do with thee, Jesus, thou Son of the most high God? I adjure thee by God, that thou torment me not. For he said unto him, Come out of the man, thou unclean spirit. And he asked him, What is thy name? And he answered, saying, My name is Legion: for we are many. And he besought him much that he would not send them away out of the country. Now there was there nigh unto the mountains a great herd of swine feeding. And all the devils besought him, saying, Send us into the swine, that we may enter into them. And forthwith Jesus gave them leave. And the unclean spirits went out, and entered into the swine: and the herd ran violently down a steep place into the sea, (they were about two thousand;) and were choked in the sea. And they that fed the swine fled, and told it in the city, and in the country. And they went out to see what it was that was done. And they come to Jesus, and see him that was possessed with the devil, and had the legion, sitting, and clothed, and in his right mind: and they were afraid. And they that saw it told them how it befell to him that was possessed with the devil, and also concerning the swine. And they began to pray him to depart out of their coasts. And when he was come into the ship, he that had been possessed with the devil prayed him that he might be with him. Howbeit Jesus suffered him not, but saith unto him, Go home to thy friends, and tell them how great things the Lord hath done for thee, and hath had compassion on thee. And he departed, and began to publish in Decapolis how great things Jesus had done for him: and all men did marvel.

GREEK WORDS

1. "immediately" — εὐθὺς (*euthus*): without delay; immediately
2. "withanuncleanspirit"—ἐνπνεύματιἀκαθάρτῳ(*enpneumatiakatharto*):in the grip of an unclean spirit; in the control of an unclean spirit
3. "unclean" — ἀκάθαρτος (*akathartos*): unclean, impure, filthy, lewd, or foul
4. "dwelling"—κατοίκησις(*katoikesis*):dwelling;habitation;residence;settled down and at home
5. "bind" — δέω (*deo*): to bind, tie up, restrict, imprison, or put in chains
6. "chains"— ἄλυσις (*halusis*): chains or handcuffs for the hands or wrists

7. "fetters" — **πέδη** (*pede*): shackles on the feet; foot chains

8. "plucked asunder" — **διασπάω** (*diaspao*): to tear in half; to sever; to tear to pieces

9. "broken in pieces" — **συντρίβω** (*suntribo*): to crush, as in crushing bones or grapes; to smash

10. "tame" — **δαμάζω** (*damadzo*): a word that means to domesticate, to subdue, or to bring under control; used to describe animal trainers who were experts at capturing and domesticating the wildest and most ferocious of beasts, such as lions, tigers, and bears; normally, these animals would maul or kill a person, but these skilled trainers were able to take the wildest animals and domesticate them

11. "crying" (v. 5), "cried" (v. 7) — **κράζω** (*kradzo*): to scream, yell, exclaim, or cry out at the top of one's voice; to shriek; pictures an urgent shout; a loud outburst of emotion

12. "cutting" — **κατακόπτω** (*katakopto*): to cut downward; to gash downward; to mutilate

13. "ran" — **τρέχω** (*trecho*): to run swiftly; to run speedily; to run without distraction

14. "worshipped" — **προσκυνέω** (*proskuneo*): to fall forward to kiss; to fall upon on one's knees in intimate adoration

15. "adjure" — **ὁρκίζω** (*horkidzo*): to solemnly plead; used in a religious sense to plead to God

16. "torment" — **βασανίζω** (*basanidzo*): to torment or torture; the form used in this verse denotes incessant torment and torture

17. "said" — **ἔλεγεν** (*elegen*): literally, "He [Jesus] kept saying..."

18. "asked" — **ἐπερωτάω** (*eperotao*): to interrogate; the tense depicts an ongoing interrogation

19. "legion" — **λεγειών** (*legion*): a military term that denoted at least 6,000 Roman soldiers

20. "many" — **πολλοί** (*polloi*): vast multitudes

21. "besought" — **παρακαλέω** (*parakaleo*): pictures one who passionately pleads or begs; a word of prayer

22. "much" — **πολλὰ** (*polla*): numerous times; over and over

23. "ran violently" — **ὁρμάω** (*hormao*): to uncontrollably and wildly rush forward

24. "choked" — **πνίγω** (*pnigo*): to choke; to strangle; to wring the neck; to take one by the throat

25. "rightmind"—σωφρονοῦντα(*sophronounta*):from σωφρονέω(*sophroneo*),pictures a delivered mind or restored intelligence (v. 15)

26. "marvel"—θαυμάζω (*thaumadzo*): to wonder; to be at a loss for words; to be shocked and amazed; to be bewildered

SYNOPSIS

Located on the eastern shore of the Sea of Galilee, there stands a monastery to commemorate a miraculous deliverance wrought by Jesus during His ministry. It was built in the Fifth Century, and it marks the place where Jesus cast out the legion of demons from the demoniac of Gadara. With persistence and compassion, He evicted thousands of unclean spirits and sent them into a pack of pigs, which ran down the steep hillside and drowned in the sea.

The emphasis of this lesson:

Once Jesus and His disciples reached the region of Gadara, a man possessed by thousands of demons ran up to Him. Although they stubbornly attempted to stay in control of the man, Jesus insisted they leave. The enemy's strength was — and is — no match for Jesus' power.

In our last lesson, Jesus and His disciples were in a boat on the Sea of Galilee heading toward the country of the Gadarenes. While en route, a massive windstorm arose and threatened their lives. It was a demonic attack designed to stop Jesus from reaching His destination. With a great display of authority and power, Jesus rebuked the wind and calmed the sea. "And they came over unto the other side of the sea, into the country of the Gadarenes" (Mark 5:1).

A difference in the details: The story of Jesus' journey to the country of the Gadarenes (sometimes referred to as Gergesenes) is found in Matthew 8, Mark 5, and Luke 8. In Matthew's account, it says two men were possessed by devils; in Mark's and Luke's tellings, only *one* man is mentioned. This is not a discrepancy in Scripture. There were two men delivered from demons. Mark and Luke chose to focus on the one who was most severely possessed.

The unclean spirit had the man: Mark 5:2 says, "And when he was come out of the ship, immediately there met him out of the tombs a man with an unclean spirit." The word "immediately" is the Greek word *euthus*, meaning *without delay; immediately*. The instant Jesus set foot on land, a man "with an unclean spirit" met Him. The Greek actually says a man "who was in the grip of" or "who was in the control of" an unclean spirit. In other words, the man didn't have an unclean spirit; the unclean spirit had the man.

The word "unclean" is the Greek word *akathartos*, and it describes *something that is unclean, impure, filthy, lewd, or foul; something sexually vulgar.* Interestingly, we are told three times that this man under the control of an unclean spirit was dwelling among the tombs (vv. 2, 3, 5). The word "dwelling," is the Greek word *katoikesis*, and it describes *a dwelling, habitation,* or *residence.* It means *to settle down and make oneself at home.* This man had settled down and made the graveyard his residence.

The significance of the tombs: The demon spirits living in this man had driven him to the brink of death. In fact, death dominated his thinking. Not only was he living in the dominion of death (among the tombs), he also desperately wanted to die. Again and again, he attempted suicide by cutting himself with stones, but he was unsuccessful at ending his life. At that point he had been living among the tombs the majority of his life.

No man could bind him: Mark 5:3 says, "…And no man could bind him, no, not with chains." The word "bind" is the Greek word *deo*, which means *to bind, tie up, restrict, imprison,* or *put in chains.* The word *deo* (bind) describes *a completed state,* which means people had tried to restrain and chain this man on previous occasions, but they couldn't keep him bound. The word "chains" here is the Greek word *halusis*, and it refers to *chains or handcuffs for the hands or wrists.*

Verse 4 continues saying "that he had been often bound with fetters and chains, and the chains had been plucked asunder by him, and the fetters broken in pieces: neither could any man tame him." In addition to chains, we see the word "fetters," which is the Greek word *pede,* and it describes *shackles on the feet, foot chains.*

This man had been handcuffed and chained around the feet many times. However, he had "plucked asunder" the chains on his hands. "Plucked asunder" is the Greek word *diaspao*, which literally means *to tear in half; to sever; to tear to pieces.* And the chains on his feet had been "broken in pieces," which is the Greek word *suntribo*, meaning *to crush, as in crushing bones or grapes; to smash.* This man was so energized by demonic powers that he was able to tear his handcuffs in half and beat his legs against each other so forcefully that the chains were crushed.

Neither could any man tame him: The word "tame" in verse 4 is the Greek word *damadzo*, and it means *to domesticate, to subdue, or to bring under control*. It was used to describe *animal trainers who were experts at capturing and domesticating the wildest and most ferocious of beasts, such as lions, tigers, and bears*. Normally, animals like these would maul or kill a person, but these skilled trainers were able to take the wildest animals and domesticate them. That is what the word "tame" means. In other words, not even the most skilled wild-animal trainers could bring this demonically possessed person under control.

He was crying and cutting himself: Mark 5:5 says, "And always, night and day, he was in the mountains, and in the tombs, crying, and cutting himself with stones." The word "crying" is the Greek word *kradzo*, which means *to scream, yell, exclaim, or cry out at the top of one's voice; to shriek*. It pictures *an urgent shout; a loud outburst of emotion*.

The word "cutting" is the Greek word *katakopto*, and it describes *a downward cut; a downward gash*; or *mutilation*. The use of this word lets us know that this miserable man was trying to commit suicide. He probably thought that was his only hope of escaping the hellish conditions he was enduring. No one could bind him in chains, and wild-animal tamers couldn't bring him under control. His condition was beyond desperate.

Then Jesus showed up: Mark 5:6 tells us, "But when he saw Jesus afar off, he ran and worshipped him…." Normally, demons don't run *to* Jesus; they run *from* Him. Yet in this case, the demon-possessed man "ran" to Jesus and "worshipped" Him.

The word "ran" is the Greek word *trecho*, which means *to run swiftly; to run speedily; to run without distraction*. This desperate man was moving his feet as fast as he could to get to Jesus. When he was in front of Him, the Bible says he "worshipped" Him. The word "worshipped" is the Greek word *proskuneo*, which means *to fall forward to kiss; to fall upon on one's knees in intimate adoration*. As soon as this man got close to Jesus, he took the posture of worship.

However, when he opened his mouth to ask Jesus for help, the demons seized control of his vocal cords and "…cried with a loud voice, and said, What have I to do with thee, Jesus, thou Son of the most high God? I adjure thee by God, that thou torment me not" (v. 7). The word "adjure" is the Greek word *horkidzo*, and it means *to solemnly plead*. It is used in a religious sense *to plead to God*. The demons were literally praying to and petitioning Jesus.

They asked Him not to "torment" them. The word "torment" is the Greek word *basanidzo*, and it describes *torment or torture*; the form used in this verse denotes *incessant torment and torture*. How was Jesus tormenting the demons? We discover the answer in verse 8.

Jesus spoke to the demon: "For he said unto him, Come out of the man, thou unclean spirit" (Mark 5:8). Notice the word "said" in this verse. It is the Greek word *elegen*, which literally means, *"He [Jesus] kept saying…."* Again and again, Jesus commanded and demanded the unclean spirit to leave. This is what was tormenting the enemy.

Normally, when Jesus delivered someone of an evil spirit, He did so with a single word. In this case, however, the unclean spirit wouldn't budge. That is why Jesus kept saying, "Come out of the man." The more Jesus commanded them come out, the more the demons shrieked aloud. Yet unlike other people who had unsuccessfully tried to help the man break free of his spiritual condition, Jesus was committed to stay with him until the demons left and he was free.

Amazed at the resistance of the unclean spirit, Jesus asked him, "What is thy name?" Jesus answered, saying, "…My name is Legion: for we are many" (Mark 5:9). The word "legion" is a military term that denoted at least 6,000 Roman soldiers. The unclean spirit in the man was saying, "There are 6,000 of us in here." This extremely large number of demons is confirmed by the use of the word "many," which is the Greek word *polloi*, meaning *vast multitudes*.

The demons pleaded with Jesus: Mark 5:10-12 says, "And he [the demon] besought him much that he would not send them away out of the country. Now there was there nigh unto the mountains a great herd of swine feeding. And all the devils besought him, saying, Send us into the swine, that we may enter into them." Initially, one demon acted as a spokesman on behalf of the thousands of demons within. But that one demonic voice quickly gave way to a concert of 6,000 demonic voices, as *all* the devils "besought" Jesus to send them into the herd of pigs.

The word "besought" is the Greek word *parakaleo*, and it pictures *one who passionately pleads or begs; a word of prayer*. Suddenly, all 6,000 demon voices began begging Jesus to give them permission to enter the pigs.

Jesus evicted the unholy horde: "And forthwith Jesus gave them leave. And the unclean spirits went out, and entered into the swine: and the herd ran violently down a steep place into the sea, (they were about two thousand;) and were choked in the sea" (Mark 5:13). Here we see that the multitude of unclean spirits were kicked out of this man and "choked" in the sea.

The word "choked" is the Greek word *pnigo*, which means *to strangle; to wring the neck; to take one by the throat; to choke to death.* This is a clear picture of the devil's ultimate goal: to steal, kill, and destroy (*see* John 10:10). Unlike human beings made in the image of God, pigs don't have a free will to resist the enemy. Therefore, when the demons entered them, they immediately self-destructed.

The results of Jesus' intervention: "And they that fed the swine fled, and told it in the city, and in the country. And they went out to see what it was that was done. And they come to Jesus, and see him that was possessed with the devil, and had the legion, sitting, and clothed, and in his right mind: and they were afraid" (Mark 5:14, 15).

The Bible says the man who had been demon-possessed was now sitting clothed and in his "right mind." The Greek here depicts a man who now has a mind that had been delivered; his intelligence had been redeemed. It is the picture of complete salvation. These are the results of a life that has been touched and transformed by Jesus.

And all who saw and heard what the Lord had done in this man did "marvel" (*see* Mark 5:20). The word "marvel" is the Greek word *thaumadzo*, which means *to wonder; to be at a loss of words; to be shocked and amazed; to be bewildered.* By delivering this man, the entire region of the Decapolis was delivered from terrorizing fear and was opened to the Good News of Jesus.

STUDY QUESTIONS

Study to shew thyself approved unto God, a workman that needeth not to be ashamed, rightly dividing the word of truth.
— 2 Timothy 2:15

1. What new insights did you learn from this account of the man with the unclean spirit?
2. According to Mark 5:18-20 and Luke 8:38, 39, once the man with the legion of demons was delivered, what was his response to Jesus? What did Jesus say in return?

3. According to God's Word, what authority and power do you have over demonic spirits? To help you answer, carefully read Luke 10:19 and 20; Matthew 16:19; and Mark 16:17.

PRACTICAL APPLICATION

> But be ye doers of the word, and not hearers only,
> deceiving your own selves.
> —James 1:22

1. Normally, when Jesus delivered someone of an evil spirit, He did so with a single word. In the case of the man with the unclean spirit, however, He *repeatedly* said, "Come out of the man" until they left. What does this say to you personally about the enemy's stubborn resistance in your own life?
2. The Bible says that when Jesus set the demoniac free, the people of the region were afraid and asked Him to leave. Why do you think they responded in this way instead of celebrating what Jesus had done? (*See* Matthew 8:33, 34; Mark 5:14-17; Luke 8:34-37.)

LESSON 11

TOPIC

Jesus Heals a Woman With an Issue of Blood

SCRIPTURES

1. **Mark 5:21-34** — And when Jesus was passed over again by ship unto the other side, much people gathered unto him: and he was nigh unto the sea. And, behold, there cometh one of the rulers of the synagogue, Jairus by name; and when he saw him, he fell at his feet, and besought him greatly, saying, My little daughter lieth at the point of death: I pray thee, come and lay thy hands on her, that she may be healed; and she shall live. And Jesus went with him; and much people followed him, and thronged him. And a certain woman, which had an issue of blood twelve years, and had suffered many things of many physicians,

and had spent all that she had, and was nothing bettered, but rather grew worse, When she had heard of Jesus, came in the press behind, and touched his garment. For she said, If I may touch but his clothes, I shall be whole. And straightway the fountain of her blood was dried up; and she felt in her body that she was healed of that plague. And Jesus, immediately knowing in himself that virtue had gone out of him, turned him about in the press, and said, Who touched my clothes? And his disciples said unto him, Thou seest the multitude thronging thee, and sayest thou, Who touched me? And he looked round about to see her that had done this thing. But the woman fearing and trembling, knowing what was done in her, came and fell down before him, and told him all the truth. And he said unto her, Daughter, thy faith hath made thee whole; go in peace, and be whole of thy plague.

GREEK WORDS

1. "issue" — ῥύσις (*rhusis*): a flowing issue; nonstop bleeding
2. "suffered" — πάσχω (*pascho*): to suffer; carries the idea of suffering, undergoing hardships, being ill-treated, or experiencing adversity; the tense means continual suffering
3. "many things" — πολλὰ (*polla*): a lot; an enormous amount
4. "of" — ὑπὸ (*hupo*): under the care of
5. "spent" — δαπανάω (*dapanao*): to incur expense; to waste or squander; pictures a wasted expense
6. "all that she had" — τὰ παρ' αὐτῆς (*ta par autes*): everything at her side; everything in her possession; everything that was available to her
7. "bettered" — ὠφεληθεῖσα (*opheletheisa*): bettered; benefited; improved
8. "worse" — χείρων (*cheiron*): worse; in this case, a sickness that is becoming more severe
9. "of" — τὰ περὶ (*ta peri*): things concerning
10. "press" — ὄχλος (*ochlus*): a crowd, a mob, or a multitude of people
11. "behind" — ὄπισθεν (*opisthen*): back; behind; from behind
12. "touched" — ἅπτομαι (*haptomai*): to lay hold of; to fasten onto
13. "said" — ἔλεγεν (*elegen*): saying repetitiously; in context, "[she] kept on saying and saying" (v. 28)
14. "shall be whole" — σωθήσομαι (*sothesomai*): the future tense of σῴζω (*sodzo*): a touch of salvation that brings delivering and healing power that results in wholeness

15. "straightway" — **εὐθὺς** (*euthus*): without delay; immediately

16. "fountain" — **πηγή** (*pege*): the idea of something that gushes; a spring or fountain

17. "felt" — **ἔγνω** (*egno*), a form of **γινώσκω** (*ginosko*): to know, perceive, or comprehend

18. "plague" — **μάστιγος** (*mastigos*): plague; a word borrowed from the world of torture that denoted the act of recurrently beating a prisoner or victim; once a person's wounds had mended, the torturers brought him back to the whipping post, where he was struck again and again and again; such beatings were sporadic but constant, and although they were not usually serious enough to kill, they kept a victim in constant pain and misery; it was torment and abuse, a scourge that caused great suffering and prolonged anguish; depicts a recurring sickness or physical affliction that keeps a sufferer in a protracted, repeated state of suffering

19. "knowing" — **ἐπίγνωσις** (*epignosis*): a well-instructed, intensive, deep knowledge of the facts; pictures one who knows his facts like a professional; someone who is very knowledgeable

20. "virtue" — **δύναμις** (*dunamis*): power; carries the idea of explosive, superhuman power that comes with enormous energy and produces phenomenal, extraordinary, and unparalleled results; the source of miraculous power or miraculous manifestations

21. "go" — **ὕπαγε** (*hupage*): to go away under someone's authority

SYNOPSIS

The city of Capernaum, also known as the city of Jesus during the First Century, was a city like no other. It was teeming with the miracles of Jesus. After He had delivered the two men of Gadara from demonic possession, including the man who was under the control of a legion of unclean spirits, He got back into the boat with His disciples and returned to Capernaum. Immediately, He was met by a swarm of people desiring to see Him and receive His healing touch. One of these people was Jairus, the ruler of the local synagogue. We will focus entirely on him in our next lesson. For now we will turn our attention to another desperate soul in the crowd — "a certain woman, which had an issue of blood twelve years" (Mark 5:25).

The emphasis of this lesson:

After 12 years of physical, financial, and emotional suffering, a woman with a nonstop bleeding issue was instantly cured when she touched the hem of Jesus' clothing. She is an example of what happens when we come into contact with the healing power of Jesus.

The Woman's Condition Was Critical

The Bible says this woman had an "issue" of blood. The word "issue" is the Greek word *rhusis*, and it describes *a flowing issue; nonstop bleeding.* What would normally start and stop each month became nonstop bleeding for 12 years. She lived in a state of physical exhaustion, and verse 26 says, "had suffered many things of many physicians, and had spent all that she had, and was nothing bettered, but rather grew worse."

The word "suffered" is the Greek word *pascho*, which means *to suffer*, and in this verse *it carries the idea of suffering, undergoing hardships, being ill-treated, or experiencing adversity.* The tense means *continual suffering.* It says she suffered "many things," which is the Greek word *polla*, meaning *a lot; an enormous amount.* The many hardships she endured were "of" many physicians. This word "of" in Greek is *hupo*, and it indicates *under the care of*, and in this case it was *under the care of the doctors.*

For years, she went from doctor to doctor, hoping and believing to find relief. It is likely that she was subjected to much experimental treatment — procedures that would be shocking and hideous by today's standards. It is not that the doctors were maliciously trying to harm her. They did all that they knew to do to try to help her, but their efforts failed.

She Spent All She Had

In the process of being a guinea pig for experimental treatments, this woman "spent all that she had." The word "spent" is the Greek word *dapanao*, which means *to incur expense; to waste or squander.* Her spending was considered a total waste since it yielded no positive results.

Also notice the phrase "all that she had." The Greek here indicates *everything at her side; everything in her possession; everything that was available to her.* And when it was all said and done, the Bible says she "was nothing bettered, but rather grew worse." The word "bettered" is the Greek word *opheletheisa*, which means *bettered; benefited; improved.* After spending every last penny, she was *not improved* but grew "worse" — the Greek word *cheiron* — which in this case describes *a sickness that is becoming more and more severe.*

She Lived in Isolation

In addition to the physical and financial pain and strain, she also endured deep emotional trauma. Having a nonstop bleeding issue for 12 years made her a social outcast in the community. According to Levitical law, she was considered unclean as long as she was bleeding (*see* Leviticus 15:19-27). Consequently, no one was to touch her, and she was to touch no one.

She was banned from sitting on the same chair with anyone or eating at the same table with others. If she was married, she couldn't touch her husband, nor could he touch her. If she had children, she was forbidden to kiss or caress them in anyway or they, too, would become unclean. This woman lived in complete isolation — totally void of the warmth of relationship.

On multiple levels, she experienced a level of misery few can comprehend. Physically and financially she was drained. Socially, she was viewed as and treated as an outcast. Having not been touched for 12 years, she was left with an emotional deficit that is indescribable. It was in this depleted and depressed condition she heard about Jesus.

Then She Heard of Jesus

Mark 5:27 says, "When she had heard of Jesus, came in the press behind, and touched his garment." Somehow on this particular day that Jesus returned to Capernaum, this woman was close enough to see and hear the crowds of people singing His praises and struggling to reach out and touch Him.

Scripture says that she heard "of" Jesus, and this word "of" is important. It is the Greek word *ta peri*, and it means *things concerning.* As this woman stood in a distant doorway, she likely heard things like, "I can see! My eyes have been opened!" and, "I can hear! My ears are healed!" and, "I can walk! Jesus restored my legs!" With each proclamation of praise she heard, faith began to arise in her heart.

She began moving forward in faith. This woman didn't have a theological degree, and she may have never heard of Jesus until that day He had returned to Capernaum from the country of the Gadarenes. Nevertheless, as she heard the cries of joy and wonder from those who had received healing, a fire of hope was ignited within. This is confirmed in Mark 5:28, which tells us, "For she said, If I may touch but his clothes, I shall be whole."

The word "said" in verse 28 is the Greek word *elegon*, which means *saying repetitiously*. In the context of this verse, *she kept on saying and saying and saying*, "If I can just get near Him… If I can make my way through this crowd… If I can just get close enough to touch His clothes, I will be made whole and this wretched bleeding will stop." The more she spoke to herself, the stronger her faith grew. With each step toward Jesus and each statement of reliance and trust in His ability to heal, her confidence expanded.

She came from behind and touched Jesus. The Bible says, "She came in the press behind." The word "press" is the Greek word *ochlus*, which describes *a crowd, a mob, or a multitude of people*, and the word "behind" indicates she came *from behind* or *from the back*. That is, she waited until the mob of people had passed, then she came up from behind and "touched" His garment.

This word "touched" is the Greek term *haptomai*, which means *to lay hold of; to fasten onto*. When she reached out to touch Jesus, she *seized* His clothing. She was reaching with everything within her for the power of God that was on Jesus, believing that she would be made "whole."

The phrase "shall be whole" in Mark 5:28 is the future tense of the Greek word *sodzo*, and it means *a touch of salvation that brings delivering and healing power that results in wholeness*. In the Jewish mindset, this is what it meant to be saved (*sodzo*), and this is what the woman with the issue of blood was reaching out to receive from Jesus.

She received her healing. "And straightway the fountain of her blood was dried up; and she felt in her body that she was healed of that plague" (Mark 5:29). The word "straightway" is the Greek word *euthus*, which means *without delay; immediately*. The word "fountain" is the Greek word *pege*, and it carries *the idea of something that gushes; a spring or fountain*. The use of this term lets us know that the woman's condition was a gushing, nonstop flow of blood.

The Bible says that the moment she touched Jesus in faith, the gushing flow "dried up," which in the Greek means it *withered away immediately*. The Scripture goes on to say, "…And she felt in her body that she was healed of that plague." The word "felt" in Greek is a form of the word *ginosko*, which means *to really know, perceive, or comprehend*. She didn't go to a doctor to have her healing verified. She just knew within herself that she had been made whole.

The plague was gone. The meaning of the word "plague" used in Mark 5:29 is quite eye-opening. It is the Greek word *mastigos*, and it is a word borrowed from the world of torture that denoted *the act of recurrently beating a prisoner or victim*. Once a person's wounds had mended, the torturers brought him back to the whipping post, where he was struck again and again. Such beatings were sporadic but constant. And although they were not usually serious enough to kill, they kept a victim in constant pain and misery. It was torment and abuse, a scourge that caused great suffering and prolonged anguish. In verse 29, this word "plague" (*mastigos*) depicts *a recurring sickness or physical affliction that keeps a sufferer in a protracted, repeated state of suffering.*

Any form of sickness that persists in you — any illness or condition that you think is gone and then comes back again and beats you down — would fall into the category of a "plague." Chronic blood pressure problems, headaches, allergies, joint issues, and stomach problems are all examples. This woman had a recurring bleeding problem for 12 years, but the moment she seized Jesus' garment, she was healed.

Jesus Knew Power Went Out of Him

Mark 5:30 says, "And Jesus, immediately knowing in himself that virtue had gone out of him, turned him about in the press, and said, Who touched my clothes?" The word "knowing" is the Greek word *epignosis*, which describes *a well-instructed, intensive, deep knowledge of the facts.* It pictures *one who knows his facts like a professional; someone who is very knowledgeable.* This tells us how aware Jesus was of the anointing on His life.

When it came to the anointing, Jesus was a professional. The moment "virtue" went out of Him, He instinctively knew it. The word "virtue" is the Greek word *dunamis*, and it carries *the idea of explosive, superhuman power that comes with enormous energy and produces phenomenal, extraordinary, and unparalleled results.* The Greek word translated *dunamis* is *the source of miraculous power or miraculous manifestations.*

Jesus said, "Who touched my clothes?" His disciples said to Him, "…Thou seest the multitude thronging thee, and sayest thou, Who touched me?…" The rest of this passage says, "…And he looked round about to see her that had done this thing. But the woman fearing and trembling, knowing what was done in her, came and fell down before him, and told him all the truth" (Mark 5:30-33).

The woman was "fearing and trembling" as a result of her knowledge of the Levitical law. Her issue of continual bleeding made her unclean, and being unclean meant she couldn't touch anyone. The fact that she touched Jesus made her guilty of a crime and gave Him the right to stone her to death. But Jesus would have never done that.

Instead, "He said unto her, Daughter, thy faith hath made thee whole; go in peace, and be whole of thy plague" (Mark 5:34). The Greek here literally says, *"Your faith has healed you."* The last word to make note of here is the word "go." It is the Greek word *hupage,* and it means *to go away under someone's authority.* Jesus released this woman to go under the power and authority of His word — and His anointing — and she went home totally cured of her plague.

STUDY QUESTIONS

Study to shew thyself approved unto God, a workman that needeth not to be ashamed, rightly dividing the word of truth.
— 2 Timothy 2:15

1. Jesus willingly went to great lengths to deliver the two demon-possessed men and heal countless people like the woman with the issue of blood. Likewise, He will go to great lengths to release His healing power in your life too. What is God's greatest demonstration of love for you? Read Romans 5:6-8 for the answer and commit it to heart.

2. One faith-building practice shown to us by the woman with the issue of blood was her choice to repeatedly speak the truth. She *kept on saying and saying,* "If I may touch but his clothes, I shall be whole" (Mark 5:27). According to Proverbs 18:20 and 21, how important are your words — including your inner self-talk? Also consider Psalm 19:14 and Philippians 4:8.

PRACTICAL APPLICATION

But be ye doers of the word, and not hearers only, deceiving your own selves.
— James 1:22

1. The woman with the issue of blood experienced suffering on many levels. It what ways can you personally identify with her? How does her story of miraculous healing encourage you?

2. Jesus called the woman's nonstop bleeding a "plague" — *a recurring sickness or physical affliction that keeps a sufferer in a protracted, repeated state of suffering.* Are you dealing with any physical challenges of this nature? If so, bring it to Jesus right now and ask Him to release His healing power (*dunamis*) into every cell of your being.

TOPIC

Jesus Raises Jairus' Daughter From Death to Life

SCRIPTURES

1. **Mark 5:21-42** — And when Jesus was passed over again by ship unto the other side, much people gathered unto him: and he was nigh unto the sea. And, behold, there cometh one of the rulers of the synagogue, Jairus by name; and when he saw him, he fell at his feet, and besought him greatly, saying, My little daughter lieth at the point of death: I pray thee, come and lay thy hands on her, that she may be healed; and she shall live. And Jesus went with him; and much people followed him, and thronged him. And a certain woman, which had an issue of blood twelve years, and had suffered many things of many physicians, and had spent all that she had, and was nothing bettered, but rather grew worse, When she had heard of Jesus, came in the press behind, and touched his garment. For she said, If I may touch but his clothes, I shall be whole. And straightway the fountain of her blood was dried up; and she felt in her body that she was healed of that plague. And Jesus, immediately knowing in himself that virtue had gone out of him, turned him about in the press, and said, Who touched my clothes? And his disciples said unto him, Thou seest the multitude thronging thee, and sayest thou, Who touched me? And he looked round about to see her that had done this thing. But the woman fearing and trembling, knowing what was done in her, came

and fell down before him, and told him all the truth. And he said unto her, Daughter, thy faith hath made thee whole; go in peace, and be whole of thy plague. While he yet spake, there came from the ruler of the synagogue's house certain which said, Thy daughter is dead: why troublest thou the Master any further? As soon as Jesus heard the word that was spoken, he saith unto the ruler of the synagogue, Be not afraid, only believe. And he suffered no man to follow him, save Peter, and James, and John the brother of James. And he cometh to the house of the ruler of the synagogue, and seeth the tumult, and them that wept and wailed greatly. And when he was come in, he saith unto them, Why make ye this ado, and weep? the damsel is not dead, but sleepeth. And they laughed him to scorn. But when he had put them all out, he taketh the father and the mother of the damsel, and them that were with him, and entereth in where the damsel was lying. And he took the damsel by the hand, and said unto her, *Talitha cumi*; which is, being interpreted, Damsel, I say unto thee, arise. And straightway the damsel arose, and walked; for she was of the age of twelve years. And they were astonished with a great astonishment.

GREEK WORDS

1. "much people" — ὄχλος πολὺς (*ochlos polus*): a massive mob of people

2. "nigh" — παρὰ (*para*): alongside, indicating Jesus could not move beyond the edge of the water

3. "rulers of the synagogue"—ἀρχισυνάγωγος (*archisunagogos*): the chief elder presiding over a local synagogue

4. "fell" — πίπτω (*pipto*): to fall; to collapse; used often to depict a person who falls so hard that it appears he has fallen dead like a corpse; a fall from a high and haughty position

5. "at" — πρὸς (*pros*): toward [Jesus' feet]

6. "besought" — παρακαλέω (*parakaleo*): to passionately call out to; to plead, to beckon, or to beg; a word of prayer

7. "lieth at the point of death"—ἐσχάτως ἔχει (*eschatos echei*): in context, she is in the last stage of her illness; she is breathing her last breaths; she doesn't have much longer to live

8. "healed" — σῴζω (*sodzo*): a touch of salvation that brings delivering and healing power that results in wholeness

9. "thronged"— **συνθλίβω** (*sunthlibo*): to crush, as to crush grapes or even bones; to crush from all sides

10. "dead"— **ἀποθνῄσκω** (*apothnesko*): in context, this tense means she has withered and wasted away; her life has expired

11. "troublest"— **σκύλλω** (*skullo*): to annoy; to vex; to flay; to skin alive

12. "heard"— **παρακούω** (*parakouo*): in context, to overhear what is said to someone else

13. "put them all out"— **ἐκβάλλω** (*ekballo*): to forcibly evict; to throw out; to expel; to drive out; to kick out; to cast out

14. "took"— **κρατέω** (*krateo*): to seize; to apprehend; pictures a masterful grip

SYNOPSIS

The miraculous healing of the woman with the issue of blood and Jairus' daughter being raised from the dead are closely interwoven in Scripture, separated in time only by hours if not minutes. Both take place in the renowned city of Capernaum just after Jesus released the two men living among the tombs from hordes of demonic spirits. It is Jairus, the well-known ruler of the synagogue, and the healing of his little girl that we will focus on in this lesson.

The emphasis of this lesson:

Jesus will go to any lengths to help those who express faith in Him. He did this for Jairus, raising his daughter back to life, and He'll do it for you, too, as you sincerely seek His face.

Jesus and His disciples arrived back in Capernaum after experiencing a ministry milestone in the country of the Gadarenes. Mark 5:21 says, "And when Jesus was passed over again by ship unto the other side, much people gathered unto him: and he was nigh unto the sea." To get a picture of what was happening here, you need to understand the meaning of some keys words.

"Much people" is the Greek phrase *ochlos polus*, and it describes *a massive mob of people*. Some have estimated that the crowd with Jesus at that time may have been the greatest multitude of people following Him up until that point. In fact, the mob was so huge that the Holy Spirit says through Mark that Jesus was "nigh unto the sea." The word "nigh" here is the Greek word *para*, and it means *alongside*. In this particular verse, it indicates that *Jesus could not move beyond the edge of the water*. When He got out of the boat, He attempted to move further onto land, but the multitude of people were pushing against Him so strongly that He was forced to stay on the edge of the sea.

Jairus Fell at Jesus' Feet

Mark 5:22 then says, "And, behold, there cometh one of the rulers of the synagogue, Jairus by name...." The fact that Jairus, a Jewish leader, was coming to Jesus was amazing. The word "behold" here confirms this. In Greek, it is the equivalent of saying, *"And wow! Can you imagine it."* By coming to Jesus for help, Jairus laid aside all religious pride and prestige and recognized the power of God operating in Jesus' life. He was also violating every religious rule, but he didn't care. His situation was desperate.

Scripture says Jairus was one of the "rulers of the synagogue." This phrase in Greek describes *the chief presiding elder among the other elders of the synagogue.* He was the head spiritual leader and was so well-known in Capernaum that the Bible introduces him as "Jairus by name." His name was included in the text because he was so well-recognized.

Verse 22 continues saying, "And when he saw him, he fell at his feet." The word "fell" is the Greek word *pipto,* which means *to fall.* In this particular verse, *pipto* means *to collapse.* It is often used to depict *a person who falls so hard that it appears that he has fallen dead like a corpse.* It is *a fall from a high and haughty position.* The Scripture says Jairus fell "at" Jesus' feet. The word "at" is the Greek word *pros,* which means *toward.* When Jairus saw Jesus, he collapsed like a dead man, hurling himself toward the feet of Jesus.

Where was Jesus at that time? He was "nigh" unto the sea. That is, He was alongside — on the very edge of the water. As Jairus, the distinguished leader of the synagogue, made his way through the crowd, the people recognized him and made a path for him to get to Jesus. Dressed in his royal robes, he rapidly approached Jesus and collapsed at His feet like a dead man.

Jairus Pleaded His Case Before Christ

There in the wet sand near the seashore, his beautiful clothing likely floating on the water, the Scripture says Jairus "besought him [Jesus] greatly, saying, My little daughter lieth at the point of death: I pray thee, come and lay thy hands on her, that she may be healed; and she shall live. And Jesus went with him; and much people followed him, and thronged him" (Mark 5:23).

The word "besought" is the Greek word *parakaleo*. It is the compound of two words: *para*, meaning *to be alongside*, and the word *kaleo*, which means *to call*. When the two words are compounded to form the word *parakaleo*, it means *to come alongside someone and passionately call out to them*. It can also be translated *to plead, to beckon, or to beg; a word of prayer*.

Jairus came alongside Jesus, collapsed at His feet, and began begging, pleading, and praying, "Come, oh please come, Jesus, and lay Your hands on my little girl." With great desperation in his voice, he explained that she "lieth at the point of death." This phrase in the Greek communicates that *she was in the last stage of her illness. She was breathing her last breaths, and she didn't have much longer to live.*

Like the woman's issue of blood, Jairus' situation was critical. He wanted to see his daughter "healed," and he believed Jesus could make that happen. The word "healed" is the Greek word *sodzo*, which is the same word we saw in our last lesson. It means *a touch of salvation that brings delivering and healing power that results in wholeness.* The Jews understood that when one receives salvation from God, it was a complete package consisting of physical, spiritual, emotional, mental, and financial restoration. *Sodzo* describes *the power of God that brings wholeness to every area of one's life.* This is the "healing" Jairus was pleading and begging Jesus to impart to his little girl.

An Interruption That Became a Miraculous Intervention

Mark 5:24 says, "And Jesus went with him; and much people followed him, and thronged him." The word "thronged" here is the Greek word *sunthlibo*, and it means *to crush, as to crush grapes or even bones; to crush from all sides.* Jesus was certainly willing to go with Jairus, but in order to accompany him, He would have to go against the grain of the crowd. Imagine the mob pushing, shoving, and screaming to get Jesus' attention and receive His healing touch. That is what Jesus was willing to endure to go with Jairus and heal his little girl.

As Jesus was en route to Jairus' home, the woman with the issue of blood came up from behind and seized the edge of Christ's clothing. Instantly, healing virtue — life-transforming power — went forth from Jesus into the broken, bleeding body of the woman, and she was made whole. Being a professional in the knowledge of healing and the anointing on His life,

Jesus recognized that power had gone out of Him and asked, "Who touched my clothes?"

Trembling in fear, knowing the dreadful consequences of being unclean and touching others, the woman fell down before Jesus and told Him all she had done. "And he said unto her, Daughter, thy faith hath made thee whole; go in peace, and be whole of thy plague" (Mark 5:34).

Jesus Told Jairus, 'Be Not Afraid, Only Believe'

In verse 35, the story quickly refocuses on Jairus and says, "While he [Jesus] yet spake, there came from the ruler of the synagogue's house certain which said, Thy daughter is dead: why troublest thou the Master any further?" The word "dead" here is the Greek word *apothnesko*, and in context, the tense means *she has withered and wasted away; her life has expired.*

The messenger then said, "Why troublest thou the Master any further?" The word "troublest" is the Greek word *skullo*, which means *to annoy; to vex; to flay; to skin alive.* The man was saying, "Why annoy or vex the Master anymore?" The messenger wasn't saying this because of Jairus' actions. He was saying it because of the crowd's actions. He was telling Jairus, "Don't put Jesus through any more of the pain of having to push through this mob to get to your house. Your daughter has breathed her last breath."

Verse 36 says, "As soon as Jesus heard the word that was spoken, he saith unto the ruler of the synagogue, Be not afraid, only believe." The word "heard" here is the Greek word *parakouo*, and in context, it means *to overhear what is said to someone else — something that was not intended to be heard.* Jesus overheard the conversation between Jairus and the messenger, and when He did, He told Jairus, "Be not afraid, only believe." In the Greek, Jesus literally said, *"Stop fearing. Be believing."* This was no time for fear; it was time for faith — the very thing that caused Jairus to seek out Jesus in the first place.

Resurrection Power Is Released
When Unbelief Is Removed

Instantly, Jesus moved into the mode of commander and took control of the situation. "And he suffered no man to follow him, save Peter, and James, and John the brother of James. And he cometh to the house of the ruler of the synagogue, and seeth the tumult, and them that wept and wailed greatly" (Mark 5:37, 38).

Notice the use of the words "tumult," "wept," and "wailed greatly." These words describe *emotions out of control that are accompanied by hysteria and loud wailing*. In those days, flute players and professional mourners were hired to make a cry of lamentation when people died. The people crying and wailing didn't know Jairus' little girl; they were just there to get paid for doing their job.

Jesus turned to the professional mourners and said, "…Why make ye this ado, and weep? the damsel is not dead, but sleepeth…." The rest of this passage says, "…And they laughed him to scorn…" (*see* Mark 5:39, 40). To the mourners, she was gone, but to Jesus, raising someone from the dead was as easy as arousing someone from sleep. He was indirectly declaring His authority over death.

Verse 40 goes on to say, "But when he had put them all out, he taketh the father and the mother of the damsel, and them that were with him, and entereth in where the damsel was lying." The phrase "put them all out" is the Greek word *ekballo*, and it means *to forcibly evict; to throw out; to expel; to drive out; to kick out; to cast out*. Jesus forcibly removed all the unbelievers. Those filled with doubt and unbelief had to go, as they would hinder the manifestation of the resurrection power needed. Peter, James, and John likely assisted in the eviction.

What happened next is nothing short of miraculous. Mark 5:41 says, "And he [Jesus] took the damsel by the hand, and said unto her, Talitha cumi; which is, being interpreted, Damsel, I say unto thee, arise." The word "took" is the Greek word *krateo*, which means *to seize; to apprehend*. It describes *a masterful grip*. Jesus seized the lifeless hand of the little girl and released the power of God into her.

"And straightway the damsel arose, and walked; for she was of the age of twelve years. And they were astonished with a great astonishment" (Mark 5:42). The phrase "astonished with a great astonishment" means *[they] had their wits completely knocked out of them*. They were so overwhelmed that they were *unable to intellectually respond*.

What Jesus did for Jairus and his family, He is still doing for families today! He is the Miracle Worker, and He is ready and able to release His supernatural power into your situation now.

STUDY QUESTIONS

**Study to shew thyself approved unto God, a workman that needeth
not to be ashamed, rightly dividing the word of truth.**
— 2 Timothy 2:15

1. Jesus told Jairus, "Stop fearing. Be Believing." Take a few moments
   to meditate on Second Timothy 1:7; Philippians 4:6,7; and First
   Peter 5:7. What do you need to *stop fearing* right now and release into
   God's hands?

2. What promises of God do you need to *be believing*? What specific
   scriptures has He given you and made alive that you need to grab hold
   of and begin meditating on and speaking?

PRACTICAL APPLICATION

But be ye doers of the word, and not hearers only,
deceiving your own selves.
— James 1:22

1. What Jesus did *then* is what He's still doing *now*. Jairus' little girl had
   died, and Jairus needed Jesus' resurrection power to bring her back to
   life. In what area(s) of your life do you need Jesus' resurrection power
   to manifest?

2. Take time now to do as Jairus did. Humble yourself before the Lord
   and "beseech" Him — *come alongside Him in prayer and call out to Him
   for help.* Pray, "Lord, release Your healing (*sodzo*) in my life and family.
   Pour out Your *salvation that brings healing and deliverance that results
   in wholeness in every area of my life.* In Jesus' name."

TOPIC

Jesus Heals a Man at the Pool of Bethesda

SCRIPTURES

1. **John 5:1-15** — After this there was a feast of the Jews; and Jesus went up to Jerusalem. Now there is at Jerusalem by the sheep market a pool, which is called in the Hebrew tongue Bethesda, having five porches. In these lay a great multitude of impotent folk, of blind, halt, withered, waiting for the moving of the water. For an angel went down at a certain season into the pool, and troubled the water: whosoever then first after the troubling of the water stepped in was made whole of whatsoever disease he had. And a certain man was there, which had an infirmity thirty and eight years. When Jesus saw him lie, and knew that he had been now a long time in that case, he saith unto him, Wilt thou be made whole? The impotent man answered him, Sir, I have no man, when the water is troubled, to put me into the pool: but while I am coming, another steppeth down before me. Jesus saith unto him, Rise, take up thy bed, and walk. And immediately the man was made whole, and took up his bed, and walked: and on the same day was the sabbath. The Jews therefore said unto him that was cured, It is the sabbath day: it is not lawful for thee to carry thy bed. He answered them, He that made me whole, the same said unto me, Take up thy bed, and walk. Then asked they him, What man is that which said unto thee, Take up thy bed, and walk? And he that was healed wist not who it was: for Jesus had conveyed himself away, a multitude being in that place. Afterward Jesus findeth him in the temple, and said unto him, Behold, thou art made whole: sin no more, lest a worse thing come unto thee. The man departed, and told the Jews that it was Jesus, which had made him whole.

GREEK WORDS

1. "pool"—**κολυμβήθρα**(*kolumbethra*):apool;ahighlysophisticated,beautiful, developed place

2. "lay" — περίκειμαι (*perikeimai*): pictures people stacked on top of people

3. "impotent(folk)"—ἀσθένεια (*astheneia*): an all-encompassing term for all types of sickness, disease, or conditions

4. "long time"—χρόνος (*chronos*): in context, a long-lasting, chronic condition

5. "whole" — ὑγιής (*hugies*): whole; healthy; pictures a normal physical condition compared to a sickly condition

6. "impotent man"— ἀσθενέω (*astheneo*): a word that generally describes a person frail in health; pictures one who is feeble, fragile, faint, incapacitated, disabled, or simply in such poor health that it would be unthinkable to transport him; a shut-in or one who is homebound; can also mean to be in financial need

7. "cured"— θεραπεύω (*therapeuo*): therapy; a healing touch that requires corresponding actions

8. "worse thing"— χείρων (*cheiron*): worse; in this case, a sickness that is becoming more severe

SYNOPSIS

Located in the city of Jerusalem is the Pool of Bethesda. In Jesus' day, it was a place of hope and healing for the frail and sick — a place where people gathered and waited to receive a supernatural touch from the Spirit of God. It was at Bethesda that a man who had been chronically sick for 38 years sat waiting to receive his miracle. That is, until Jesus showed up and performed a miracle that totally changed his life.

The emphasis of this lesson:

The lame man had been waiting at the Pool of Bethesda for 38 years to make it into the water and receive his healing — when suddenly he encountered Jesus and was instantly made whole.

The History Behind Bethesda

Our journey begins in John 5:1 and 2, which says, "After this there was a feast of the Jews; and Jesus went up to Jerusalem. Now there is at Jerusalem by the sheep market a pool, which is called in the Hebrew tongue Bethesda, having five porches." Notice the word "pool." It is the Greek word *kolumbethra*, and it describes *a pool; a highly sophisticated, beautiful, developed place*. It is actually the same word that is used to describe the Pool of Siloam (*see* John 9:7-11).

Originally, Bethesda was a beautiful pool covered with marble, decorated by stunning frescoes, and perhaps featured mosaics on the walls and floor. When it was first developed, it was the gathering place for the rich, the well-educated, the priesthood, and the intelligentsia of Jerusalem. However, over time this very expensive, well-developed piece of property fell into disrepair.

In addition to the facility becoming run down, the water source began to dry up. What was once a life-giving, flowing spring became stagnant, still water. The intense heat of the region turned the pool disgustingly pungent, causing the wealthy and elite to abandon it and go elsewhere. As they moved out, sick people began moving in to take their place.

Interestingly, Bethesda was not the name of this pool when it opened. It was renamed "Bethesda" by the sick. "Bethesda" means "The House of Mercy," and that is how countless individuals viewed the pool — *the place where God's mercy was poured out*.

A Multitude Waited for the Troubling of the Water

Five porches surrounded this pool of water, all of which were covered with colonnades or porticos. "In these lay a great multitude of impotent folk, of blind, halt, withered, waiting for the moving of the water" (John 5:3). The word "lay" in this verse is the Greek word *perikeimai*, which pictures *people stacked on top of people*. One sick person was next to another sick person who was next to another sick person. They could hardly move as a result of the multitude lying all around the place.

The Scripture says the people there were "impotent," which is the Greek word *astheneia — an all-encompassing term for all types of sickness, disease, or conditions*. All these "impotent" folk were waiting for the moving of the water. "For an angel went down at a certain season into the pool, and troubled the water: whosoever then first after the troubling of the water stepped in was made whole of whatsoever disease he had" (John 5:4).

The word "troubled" in Greek means *to agitate or stir; it was a circular movement of the water which resulted in a sudden fierce spinning that went round and round inside the pool*. Since the spring had dried up and there was no water flowing into or out of the pool, there was no natural explanation for such movement in the water. Therefore, the people believed an angel came and did it.

Jesus Asked, 'Do You Really Want to Get Well?'

John 5:5 says, "And a certain man was there, which had an infirmity thirty and eight years." It is safe to say that when this man had first begun going to the pool 38 years earlier, he went in faith, believing he could be made whole. He had heard that God's mercy was being poured out in "Bethesda" and wanted to experience it himself. All the sick that were there had heard of the miraculous healings that occurred when the angel came and stirred the water and someone stepped into it. Each one wanted to be the first to make it into the pool so he or she could be healed.

After nearly four decades of waiting and watching, he had undoubtedly seen many miracles. It's possible he even witnessed a number of his friends and neighbors get healed. Nevertheless, he was still lying there sick, waiting for *his* opportunity to receive *his* miracle.

Then in walked Jesus. "When Jesus saw him lie, and knew that he had been now a long time in that case, he saith unto him, Wilt thou be made whole?" (John 5:6). The phrase "long time" is the Greek word *chronos*, which in context means *a long-lasting, chronic condition.* This man had been physically lying there for a long time, and when Jesus saw him, He diagnosed that the man was also "lying down" inwardly. That is, mentally, emotionally, and spiritually, he had given up.

Jesus asked him, "Wilt thou be made whole?" The word "whole" here is the Greek word *hugies*, which means *whole and healthy; it pictures a normal physical condition compared to a sickly condition.* Jesus asked the man, "Do you really want to get well?" Although this may seem like a strange question to ask someone who had been sick and waiting to be healed for 38 years, it was actually quite significant.

Sickness Had Become His Identity

After such a long time of waiting and wallowing in the same sick situation, the man had adapted to his circumstances. Being sick was normal, and in a certain way, his infirmity had become his identity. He thought and acted like a sick person. All of his friends at the Pool of Bethesda were sick people, and every conversation they had was about the declining state of health each of them was enduring.

If this man were to be healed, many things in his life would instantly change. For 38 years, someone had been graciously taking care of him, including paying his bills. Once he was healed, he would have to assume these responsibilities. This would require him to get a job and possibly secure more education or training. He would also have to find new friends as he couldn't keep his sick friends and simultaneously become a healthy member of society.

Thus, when Jesus asked the man, "Do you really want to get well?" He was asking him, "Are you ready and willing to change? Do you really want Me to radically transform everything in your life?" Receiving his healing wasn't just about feeling better. For Jesus, to heal him meant this man would have to take on a whole new way of life.

Many people today say they want to change and want to experience Jesus' miracle-working power in their lives — until they understand what it will require of them. They've grown accustomed to their dysfunctional relationships. They've adapted to and accepted their sickness or difficult financial situation as normal. To leave these things would be to leave what they understand and that with which they have grown comfortable.

Jesus Saw Beyond the Man's Confusion and Condition

How did the man answer Jesus' direct question? John 5:7 says, "The impotent man answered him, Sir, I have no man, when the water is troubled, to put me into the pool: but while I am coming, another steppeth down before me." The man offered a detailed excuse as to why he was still sick and sitting by the pool. He said, "Well, I would like to be healed, *but….*"

The phrase "impotent man" in this verse is the Greek word *astheneo*, and it generally describes *a person frail in health*. It pictures *one who is feeble, fragile, faint, incapacitated, disabled, or simply in such poor health that it would be unthinkable to transport him*. The word *astheneo* can also refer to *a shut-in or one who is homebound* or *one who is in financial need*.

Thankfully, Jesus saw beyond the man's confusion and into his heart. He knew that the man had been there for 38 years and he really wanted to be healed. Although he had lost hope, he had come there in faith, believing and desiring to be healed. With this knowledge, "Jesus saith unto him, Rise, take up thy bed, and walk…." The rest of this passage says, "…And immediately the man was made whole, and took up his bed, and walked: and on the same day was the sabbath" (John 5:9, 10).

A Religious Spirit Blinds Us to God's Grace

This healing took place on the Sabbath, so when the man took up his bed as Jesus had instructed, the Jews took up an offense with him. "The Jews therefore said unto him that was cured, It is the sabbath day: it is not lawful for thee to carry thy bed. He answered them, He that made me whole, the same said unto me, Take up thy bed, and walk" (John 5:10, 11).

Just imagine. This man had been waiting 38 years to be healed. Finally, the miraculous and merciful hand of God through Jesus healed him, and the Jews erupted in protest. Instead of seeing God's goodness, they saw this man violating the Sabbath. It was as if they said, "What are you doing? This is not a convenient time for you to be healed. Put your mat down and get back on it."

When God does a miracle in your life, not everyone around you will share in your joy. Those who are religious and focused on following the rules will resist change at every turn — even if the change is a supernatural healing.

The Bible says that this man had been "cured," which is the Greek word *therapeuo*, the word from which we get "therapy." It is the primary word used in the gospels to explain the healing ministry of Jesus. *Therapeuo* — here translated "cured" — describes *a healing touch that requires corresponding actions*. It means Jesus didn't just release power; He required people to do something to cooperate with and confirm the healing process.

In this case, Jesus told the man lying at the pool to take up his bed and walk. When the man obeyed Jesus' instruction, the power of God took root in him, and he was completely healed. After 38 years, this man's time had finally come. Your time has come too!

STUDY QUESTIONS

> **Study to shew thyself approved unto God, a workman that needeth
> not to be ashamed, rightly dividing the word of truth.**
> **— 2 Timothy 2:15**

1. Although God will require us to cooperate with Him to experience our breakthrough, we must never forget that He is the One who brings about positive change in our lives. Take a few moments to reflect on Philippians 1:6; 2:12 and 13; and First Thessalonians 5:23

and 24. What do these verses say to you about God's role in the process of transformation?

2. Remember the definition of *therapeuo*? It's *a healing touch that requires corresponding actions*. Sometimes God will ask us to do things in the healing process that don't make sense. Check out the story of Naaman and Elisha in Second Kings 5 for a classic example. What did Elisha tell Naaman to do to receive his healing? How would you have reacted if you'd been given those instructions?

PRACTICAL APPLICATION

> But be ye doers of the word, and not hearers only,
> deceiving your own selves.
> —James 1:22

1. Like the man at the Pool of Bethesda, have you been waiting and believing for a mighty move of God to bring a miracle into your life? If so, what is it?

2. Has your infirmity become your identity? Have you so adapted to your difficult circumstances that you have lost the hope and belief that things will change?

3. As Jesus asked the man at the Pool of Bethesda, He now asks you: "Do you really want to be healed? Are you ready and willing to cooperate with the power of God and make the changes that are required to experience your miracle?"

LESSON 14

TOPIC

Jesus Raises Lazarus From the Dead

SCRIPTURES

1. **John 11:1-6** — Now a certain man was sick, named Lazarus, of Bethany, the town of Mary and her sister Martha. (It was that Mary which anointed the Lord with ointment, and wiped his feet with her hair, whose brother Lazarus was sick.) Therefore his sisters sent unto him, saying, Lord, behold, he whom thou lovest is sick. When Jesus

heard that, he said, This sickness is not unto death, but for the glory of God, that the Son of God might be glorified thereby. Now Jesus loved Martha, and her sister, and Lazarus. When he had heard therefore that he was sick, he abode two days still in the same place where he was.

2. **John 11:11-14** — ... After that he saith unto them, Our friend Lazarus sleepeth; but I go, that I may awake him out of sleep. Then said his disciples, Lord, if he sleep, he shall do well. Howbeit Jesus spake of his death: but they thought that he had spoken of taking of rest in sleep. Then said Jesus unto them plainly, Lazarus is dead.

3. **John 11:17** — Then when Jesus came, he found that he had lain in the grave four days already.

4. **John 11:19-44** — And many of the Jews came to Martha and Mary, to comfort them concerning their brother. Then Martha, as soon as she heard that Jesus was coming, went and met him: but Mary sat still in the house. Then said Martha unto Jesus, Lord, if thou hadst been here, my brother had not died. But I know, that even now, whatsoever thou wilt ask of God, God will give it thee. Jesus saith unto her, Thy brother shall rise again. Martha saith unto him, I know that he shall rise again in the resurrection at the last day. Jesus said unto her, I am the resurrection, and the life: he that believeth in me, though he were dead, yet shall he live. And whosoever liveth and believeth in me shall never die. Believest thou this? She saith unto him, Yea, Lord: I believe that thou art the Christ, the Son of God, which should come into the world. And when she had so said, she went her way, and called Mary her sister secretly, saying, The Master is come, and calleth for thee. As soon as she heard that, she arose quickly, and came unto him. Now Jesus was not yet come into the town, but was in that place where Martha met him. The Jews then which were with her in the house, and comforted her, when they saw Mary, that she rose up hastily and went out, followed her, saying, She goeth unto the grave to weep there. Then when Mary was come where Jesus was, and saw him, she fell down at his feet, saying unto him, Lord, if thou hadst been here, my brother had not died. When Jesus therefore saw her weeping, and the Jews also weeping which came with her, he groaned in the spirit, and was troubled. And said, Where have ye laid him? They said unto him, Lord, come and see. Jesus wept. Then said the Jews, Behold how he loved him! And some of them said, Could not this man, which opened the eyes of the blind, have caused that even this

man should not have died? Jesus therefore again groaning in himself cometh to the grave. It was a cave, and a stone lay upon it. Jesus said, Take ye away the stone. Martha, the sister of him that was dead, saith unto him, Lord, by this time he stinketh: for he hath been dead four days. Jesus saith unto her, Said I not unto thee, that, if thou wouldest believe, thou shouldest see the glory of God? Then they took away the stone from the place where the dead was laid. And Jesus lifted up his eyes, and said, Father, I thank thee that thou hast heard me. And I knew that thou hearest me always: but because of the people which stand by I said it, that they may believe that thou hast sent me. And when he thus had spoken, he cried with a loud voice, Lazarus, come forth. And he that was dead came forth, bound hand and foot with graveclothes: and his face was bound about with a napkin. Jesus saith unto them, Loose him, and let him go.

GREEK WORDS

1. "sick"—ἀσθενέω (*astheneo*): a word that generally describes a person frail in health; to be so physically weak that one is unable to travel; pictured those who were feeble, fragile, faint, incapacitated, disabled, or simply in such poor health that it would be unthinkable to transport them; also pictures shut-ins or those who are homebound

2. "death" — θάνατος (*thanatos*): physical death

3. "dead" — ἀποθνῄσκω (*apothnesko*): to wither away; to waste away; to slowly die; to expire

4. "ask" — αἰτέω (*aiteo*): to request, beseech, petition, or demand; to be adamant in requesting assistance to meet tangible needs, such as food, shelter, money, or other physical needs; firmly requesting that a need be met; asking with full expectation to receive what is being firmly requested

5. "resurrection" — ἀνάστασις (*anastasis*): a standing or rising again; a rising from the dead; resurrection

6. "weeping" — κλαίω (*klaio*): mourning, weeping, or grieving

7. "groaned" (v. 33), "groaning" (v. 38) — ἐμβριμάομαι (*embrimaomai*): to be moved with anger; to be moved with indignation; enraged; also, to snort, like an angry horse

8. "troubled" — ταράσσω (*tarasso*): to agitate; to deeply anger; to deeply disturb; to stir up

9. "wept" — δακρύω (*dakruo*): pictures an abrupt release of tears; to burst into tears; to sob

10. "stinketh" — ὄζω (*odzo*): to offensively stink; pictures the smell of a decaying corpse

11. "criedwithaloudvoice"—φωνῇμεγάλῃἐκραύγασεν(*phonemegaleekraugasen*): to yell, scream, or cry out with a very loud voice

12. "loose" — λύω (*luo*): to loose; to set free

13. "let him go" — ὑπάγω (*hupago*): to go under [Jesus'] authority (v. 44)

SYNOPSIS

Located on the outskirts of Jerusalem is the ancient city of Bethany. It was home to some of Jesus' most dearly loved friends — Mary and Martha, who were sisters, and their brother Lazarus. Toward the very end of Jesus' ministry, Lazarus became sick and died. Jesus arrived in Bethany four days after Lazarus had been buried. There Jesus performed one of His greatest miracles. Standing before the entrance to his tomb, Jesus called out to Lazarus with a loud voice and raised him back to life.

The emphasis of this lesson:

For Jesus, rousing someone from death is just as easy as rousing them from sleep. He clearly demonstrated that He is the Resurrection and the Life when He raised Lazarus from the grave. Jesus' power is *stand-again power*!

Jesus Received News of Lazarus' Sickness

The story of Lazarus is recorded in John chapter 11, starting in verse 1. "Now a certain man was sick, named Lazarus, of Bethany, the town of Mary and her sister Martha. (It was that Mary which anointed the Lord with ointment, and wiped his feet with her hair, whose brother Lazarus was sick.) Therefore his sisters sent unto him, saying, Lord, behold, he whom thou lovest is sick. When Jesus heard that, he said, This sickness is not unto death, but for the glory of God, that the Son of God might be glorified thereby. Now Jesus loved Martha, and her sister, and Lazarus. When he had heard therefore that he was sick, he abode two days still in the same place where he was" (John 11:1-6).

In these six verses, the word "sick" is mentioned five times. It is the Greek word *astheneo*, and it describes *a person frail in health; to be so physically weak that one is unable to travel.* The word *astheneo* is *a picture of those who were feeble, fragile, faint, incapacitated, disabled, or simply in such poor health that it would be unthinkable to transport them.* It also pictures *shut-ins or people who are homebound.*

When Jesus received news that His friend Lazarus was homebound and incapacitated, He wanted to go to him immediately, but He didn't. Instead He stayed where He was for two more days. On the surface, His actions didn't make sense, but we must remember He was being led by the Holy Spirit.

The Spirit knew that Jesus' enemies had gathered in Bethany, sure He would come to visit His trusted but sick friend. They were waiting for Him to arrive so they could stone Him to death. Two days later, when His enemies had dropped their stones and gone home, Jesus was released in His spirit to go to Bethany.

Lazarus Was Dead

John 11:11-13 says, "Our friend Lazarus sleepeth; but I go, that I may awake him out of sleep. Then said his disciples, Lord, if he sleep, he shall do well. Howbeit Jesus spake of his death: but they thought that he had spoken of taking of rest in sleep."

When Jesus said Lazarus was sleeping, the disciples thought He meant Lazarus was resting and on the mend, but that was not the case. Lazarus had indeed died, which is confirmed in verses 13 and 14. The word "death" in verse 13 is the Greek word *thanatos*, which describes *physical death.* Jesus was fully aware that Lazarus had physically passed away.

To make sure the disciples understood this, He told them plainly in verse 14, "…Lazarus is dead." The Greek word for "dead" here is *apothnesko*, which means *to wither away; to waste away; to slowly die; to expire.* Nevertheless, neither sleep nor death mattered to Jesus. He could arouse someone from death just as easily as He could arouse him from sleep.

Jesus Talked With Martha

John 11:17 says, "…When Jesus came, he found that he [Lazarus] had lain in the grave four days already." The word "grave" in this verse is the Greek word for an ancient tomb. It was not the type of grave you would find in a cemetery today. This was a deep cave with steps that led down to a lower chamber where Lazarus' body was laid.

As Jesus was making His way toward town, Martha went out and met Him, but Mary stayed at home. "Then said Martha unto Jesus, Lord, if thou hadst been here, my brother had not died. But I know, that even now, whatsoever thou wilt ask of God, God will give it thee" (John 11:21, 22).

Notice the word "ask" in verse 22. It is the Greek word *aiteo*, and it means *to request, beseech, strongly petition, or demand; to be adamant in requesting assistance to meet tangible needs, such as food, shelter, money, or other physical needs.* It indicates *firmly requesting that a need be met; asking with full expectation to receive what is being firmly requested.* Martha had an unshakable confidence in Jesus' ability because she had seen Him "ask" the Father for certain things on previous occasions, and He received them.

"Jesus saith unto her, Thy brother shall rise again. Martha saith unto him, I know that he shall rise again in the resurrection at the last day. Jesus said unto her, I am the resurrection, and the life: he that believeth in me, though he were dead, yet shall he live" (John 11:23-25).

In this passage, Jesus said He is the "resurrection," which is the Greek word *anastasis*. It is the compound of two words: *ana*, which means *to do something again*, and the word *stasis*, which means *to stand*. When these two words are combined to form the word *anastasis*, it means *a standing or rising again; a rising from the dead; resurrection.* What Jesus was saying here is, "I am stand-again power. I have the power to put anyone back on their feet — even someone who is dead."

John 11:26-28 says, "And whosoever liveth and believeth in me shall never die. Believest thou this? She [Martha] saith unto him, Yea, Lord: I believe that thou art the Christ, the Son of God, which should come into the world. And when she had so said, she went her way, and called Mary her sister secretly, saying, The Master is come, and calleth for thee."

Jesus 'Groaned' and Was 'Troubled'

As soon as Mary made it to where Jesus was, she collapsed at His feet and said, "...Lord, if thou hadst been here, my brother had not died. When Jesus therefore saw her weeping, and the Jews also weeping which came with her, he groaned in the spirit, and was troubled" (John 11:32, 33).

There are three very important words in this passage you need to understand. The first is "weeping," which is the Greek word *klaio*, and it means *mourning, weeping, or grieving.* When Jesus saw the uncontrollable *mourning* and *grieving* of Mary and the Jews that were with her, He "groaned" in His spirit. This word "groaned" in the Greek means *to be moved with anger; to be moved with indignation; enraged.* It is the same Greek word that describes *an angry horse that is snorting and terrifying people.*

The third word to take note of in John 11:33 is "troubled." It is the Greek word *tarasso*, and it means *to agitate; to deeply anger; to deeply disturb; or to stir up.* By using the words "groaned" and "troubled," we know that Jesus was filled with divine anger and indignation deep within. Like an angry horse, He was snorting against the spirit of death and against unbelief. Remember, Martha and Mary had both said, "Lord, if You had been here, this wouldn't have happened." They placed a degree of blame at Jesus' feet for the death of their brother Lazarus, thus demonstrating that unbelief was operating in their lives.

'Jesus Wept'

Jesus was deeply disturbed and agitated with all that He was seeing and hearing. John 11:34-36 says, "Where have ye laid him? They said unto him, Lord, come and see. Jesus wept. Then said the Jews, Behold how he loved him!"

The shortest verse in the Bible — "Jesus wept" — is also one of the most misunderstood verses. "Jesus wept" doesn't mean He was overwhelmed with emotion over the death of Lazarus. The word "wept" is the Greek word *dakruo*, and it depicts *an abrupt release of tears; to burst into tears; or to sob. This is a torrent of emotion released from deep inside.*

To understand what Jesus was so intensely emotional about, we have to look back at the verses that precede verse 35. Specifically, we need to review verse 33. Remember, Jesus "groaned" when He saw Mary and the Jews weeping — He was *moved with anger and indignation and was enraged* over the people's unbelief. Scripture also says He was "troubled" — the Greek word *tarasso*, meaning *agitated; deeply angered; deeply disturbed.* The reason "Jesus wept," displaying such a torrent of emotions from deep within, was a result of the power of God in Him rising up against the spirit of death and against unbelief.

We see this dynamic continuing to build in verses 37 and 38: "And some of them said, Could not this man, which opened the eyes of the blind, have caused that even this man should not have died? Jesus therefore again groaning in himself cometh to the grave. It was a cave, and a stone lay upon it." Here again we see the word "groaning" — the same Greek word, which means *to be moved with anger; to be moved with indignation; to be enraged; to snort, like an angry horse.*

Jesus Raised Lazarus Back to Life

Now standing at the mouth of the tomb, "Jesus said, Take ye away the stone. Martha, the sister of him that was dead, saith unto him, Lord, by this time he stinketh: for he hath been dead four days" (John 11:39). The word "stinketh" is the Greek word *odzo*, which means *to offensively stink.* It pictures *the smell of a decaying corpse.* After four days of death at work, Lazarus' body would have emitted a foul odor.

Nevertheless, "Jesus saith unto her, Said I not unto thee, that, if thou wouldest believe, thou shouldest see the glory of God? Then they took away the stone from the place where the dead was laid. And Jesus lifted up his eyes, and said, Father, I thank thee that thou hast heard me. And I knew that thou hearest me always: but because of the people which stand by I said it, that they may believe that thou hast sent me. And when he thus had spoken, he cried with a loud voice, Lazarus, come forth" (John 11:40-43).

It's important to note that Jesus was not standing far away from the tomb; He was directly in front of the entrance to this cave, speaking loudly down into it. Scripture says He "cried with a loud voice," which is from the Greek phrase *phone megale ekraugasen,* meaning *to yell, scream, or cry out with a very loud voice.* When Jesus cried out, "Lazarus, come forth," the Bible says, "And he that was dead came forth, bound hand and foot with graveclothes: and his face was bound about with a napkin. Jesus saith unto them, Loose him, and let him go" (John 11:44).

The word "loose" is the Greek term *luo,* which means *to loose; to set free.* And the phrase "let him go" is the Greek word *hupago* — the same word we have seen repeatedly used in the stories of Jesus' miracles. The word *hupago* means *to go under; to go under my authority.* Lazarus was raised back to life by the word of power spoken by Jesus, and under the power and authority of His word, he returned home to live his life.

That is the power of God's Word. It can raise the dead, and can raise you out of the dead situation you are in and bring you into new life.

STUDY QUESTIONS

Study to shew thyself approved unto God, a workman that needeth not to be ashamed, rightly dividing the word of truth.
— 2 Timothy 2:15

1. What new insights is the Holy Spirit showing you in the miraculous account of Lazarus being raised from the dead?

2. Jesus' decision to wait two days before going to Bethany was prompted by the Holy Spirit. Sometimes the Spirit speaks a clear word of direction; at times, we are directed by the *presence* or *absence* of something very important. Read Colossians 3:15 and identify this vital element. (Also consider Luke 1:78, 79; John 14:27; Psalm 29:11.)

3. God's Word is filled with promises concerning this life-giving virtue. Take time to reflect on Isaiah 26:3 and 4; Philippians 4:6-8; and First Peter 3:10 and 11. According to these passages, what part do you play in receiving and experiencing this priceless gift?

PRACTICAL APPLICATION

But be ye doers of the word, and not hearers only, deceiving your own selves.
— James 1:22

Mary and Martha sent word to Jesus that Lazarus was sick so that He would come and heal him. This was their *prayer*. But Jesus purposely waited two more days before responding to their request.

1. Have you prayed and asked God to come to your aid and He seemed distant and unresponsive? If so, briefly describe your request and situation.

2. How does knowing the outcome of this story — that Jesus received *greater glory* from raising Lazarus from the grave than just healing him — help you trust God through delays?

3. The death of Lazarus certainly seemed hopeless to his sisters, but things didn't stay that way. If your hopes have died while waiting for Jesus to show up, don't give up! God has an even greater miracle He desires to

bring about in your life. Take time to ponder Ephesians 3:20 and imagine what the Lord has in store for you.

LESSON 15

TOPIC

Jesus Restores Malchus' Ear and Raises a Boy From the Dead

SCRIPTURES

1. **John 18:3-6** — Judas then, having received a band of men and officers from the chief priests and Pharisees, cometh thither with lanterns and torches and weapons. Jesus therefore, knowing all things that should come upon him, went forth, and said unto them, Whom seek ye? They answered him, Jesus of Nazareth. Jesus saith unto them, I am he.... As soon then as he had said unto them, I am he, they went backward, and fell to the ground.

2. **Exodus 3:14** — And God said unto Moses, I AM THAT I AM: and he said, Thus shalt thou say unto the children of Israel, I AM hath sent me unto you.

3. **John 8:58** — Verily, verily, I say unto you, Before Abraham was, I am.

4. **Luke 22:49** ...Lord, shall we smite with the sword?

5. **John 18:10** — The Simon Peter having a sword drew it, and smote the high priest's servant, and cut off his right ear. The servant's name was Malchus.

6. **Mark 14:51, 52** — And there followed him a certain young man, having a linen cloth cast about his naked body; and the young men laid hold on him: and he left the linen cloth, and fled from them naked.

GREEK WORDS

1. "a band of men" — **σπεῖρα** (*speira*): a military cohort; a tenth of a legion; approximately 600 soldiers; well-trained soldiers who were equipped with the finest weaponry of the day

2. "officers"— **ὑπηρέτης** (*huperetes*): the "police officers" who worked on the temple grounds

3. "a great multitude of soldiers" — **ὄχλος πολὺς** (*ochlos polus*): a huge or massive crowd; a multitude (*see* Matthew 26:47)

4. "a great multitude"— **ὄχλος** (*ochlos*): a massive crowd (*see* Mark 14:43)

5. "a multitude"— **ὄχλος** (*ochlos*): indicating that the band of soldiers who came that night was enormous (*see* Luke 22:47)

6. "I am" — **Ἐγώ εἰμι** (*Ego eimi*): "I AM!"

7. "went backward"— **ἀπέρχομαι** (*aperchomai*): depicts the soldiers and temple police staggering and stumbling backward, as if some force had hit them and was pushing them back and down

8. "fell" — **πίπτω** (*pipto*): to fall; depicts a person who falls so hard that it appears he has fallen dead or has fallen like a corpse

9. "to the ground"— **χαμαί** (*chamai*): depicts falling abruptly and hitting the ground hard

10. "smite"— **πατάσσω** (*patasso*): to strike with the intention to kill

11. "smote"— **παίω** (*paio*): to strike, as a person who viciously strikes someone with a dangerous tool, weapon, or instrument; in this verse, it pictures the force of Peter's swinging action

12. "cut off"— **ἀποκόπτω** (*apokopto*): a downward swing that severs something; also, to castrate

13. "ear"— **ὠτίον** (*otion*): refers to the entire outer ear

14. "touched"— **ἅπτομαι** (*haptomai*): to firmly grasp or to hold tightly; to aggressively touch

15. "healed"— **ἰάομαι** (*iaomai*): to cure, to restore, or to heal

16. "linen cloth"— **σινδών** (*sindon*): used in the New Testament only to depict a linen cloth in which individuals were wrapped for burial; thus, it is a burial shroud that was used for covering a dead body in the grave

SYNOPSIS

The garden of Gethsemane was immense at the time of Jesus, covering nearly the entire slope of the Mount of Olives. In addition to the orchard of olive trees, Gethsemane was also home to a cemetery filled with graves as well as a unique arrangement of caves known as the Grotto of Gethsemane. It was in this backdrop that the final scenes of Jesus life and ministry played out — the place where once again His miraculous power was displayed in unprecedented form.

The emphasis of this lesson:

Jesus' miraculous power was legendary. In His final hours, He declared His deity and knocked hundreds of soldiers to the ground; He fully restored the castrated ear of the high priest's servant, and He raised a dead boy back to life. Wherever Jesus went, His power was manifested.

A Multitude of Armed Men Gathered in Gethsemane

Our lesson opens in the garden of Gethsemane the night Jesus was betrayed. John 18:3 says, "Judas then, having received a band of men and officers from the chief priests and Pharisees, cometh thither with lanterns and torches and weapons." In most people's minds, Judas came to the garden with a handful of soldiers, but that was not the case. The phrase "a band of men" confirms this. It is the Greek word *speira*, and it describes *a military cohort,* which is *a tenth of a legion or approximately 600 soldiers. These were well-trained soldiers who were equipped with the finest weaponry of the day.*

Not only were there 600 soldiers with Judas, but also "officers," which is the Greek word *huperetes,* and it describes *the "police officers" who worked on the temple grounds* and defended them from rebellious uprisings. These soldiers and brutal temple officers were well-trained and well-equipped. In fact, the Scripture says they came that night with "weapons" — the Greek word *hoplon,* which described *the full weaponry of a Roman soldier when he is called into combat.* The only reason they would have had their full weaponry is because they anticipated the need to use it.

Make no mistake; there was a multitude of armed men that came to Gethsemane to arrest Jesus. Matthew 26:47 describes it as "a great multitude of soldiers," which is the Greek words *ochlos polus,* meaning *a huge or massive crowd; a multitude.* Mark 14:43 says Judas came with "a great multitude" — the Greek word *ochlos,* which means *a massive crowd.* And Luke 22:47 tells us that a "multitude" accompanied Judas. Again, this is the Greek word *ochlos,* indicating that *the band of soldiers who came that night was enormous.*

Jesus Identified Himself As 'I AM!'

As the mob of militia arrived to arrest Jesus, He said to them, "Whom seek ye?" The rest of that passage says, "... They answered him Jesus of Nazareth.

Jesus saith unto them, I am he…" (John 18:4, 5). The words "I am" are the Greek words *Ego eimi*, which means *"I AM!"* These are the exact words God used to describe Himself to Moses in Exodus 3:14. "I AM THAT I AM… Thus shalt thou say unto the children of Israel, I AM hath sent me unto you."

This wasn't the first time Jesus referred to Himself as "I am" — *Ego eimi*. He did so in John 13:19, and in John 8:58 He said, "Verily, verily, I say unto you, Before Abraham was, I AM."

When Jesus said, "I am," it was the equivalent of Him saying, "I am the God of the Old Testament." John 18: 6 says, "As soon then as he had said unto them, I am he, they went backward, and fell to the ground." When Jesus uttered those words, a blast of divine power was released, and more than 600 soldiers and officers "went backward, and fell to the ground."

The words "went backward" is the Greek word *aperchomai*, and *it depicts the soldiers and temple police staggering and stumbling backward, as if some force had hit them and was pushing them back and down.* The word "fell" is the Greek word *pipto*, which means *to fall,* but it also depicts *a person who falls so hard that it appears he has fallen dead or has fallen like a corpse.* And the phrase "to the ground" is the Greek word *chamai*, which *depicts falling abruptly and hitting the ground really hard.*

Imagine the scene: six hundred Roman soldiers plus temple police officers march up to Jesus to take Him into custody. He spoke two words — "I am" — and they were all flattened to the ground under the power of God!

Peter Swung Into Action

As the armed men lay on the ground dazed and dumbfounded by God's power, Peter recognized one person in particular whom he absolutely despised. It was Malchus, the servant of Caiaphas the high priest. Whenever Caiaphas wanted to verbally assassinate people, he would voice his message through Malchus. As the mouthpiece, Malchus had spewed many poisonous accusations about Jesus and His disciples, and Peter couldn't stand him. When he saw Malchus lying on the ground, he seized the opportunity to take revenge.

Luke 22:49 says that Peter turned to Jesus and said, "Lord, shall we smite with the sword?" The word "smite" here is the Greek word *patasso*, and it means *to strike with the intention to kill.* This lets us know that when Peter swung the sword at Malchus, he intended to kill him.

The apostle John records the event saying, "Then Simon Peter having a sword drew it, and smote the high priest's servant, and cut off his right ear. The servant's name was Malchus" (John 18:10). The word "smote" in this verse is the Greek word *paio*, which means *to strike, as a person who viciously strikes someone with a dangerous tool, weapon, or instrument.* In this verse, it pictures *the force of Peter's swinging action.*

Peter was aiming for Malchus' head but only managed to "cut off his right ear." The phrase "cut off" is the Greek word *apokopto*, which describes *a downward swing that severs something.* It is the same Greek word used to describe the process of *castration.* The word "ear" is the Greek word *otion*, which refers to *the entire outer ear.*

Jesus Cleaned Up Peter's Mess

Peter's reckless use of the sword really made a mess of things. Although Jesus didn't need Peter's help to defend Himself, Peter definitely needed Jesus' help. He had assaulted a high-profile public official with a deadly weapon. His actions warranted being arrested, placed on trial, locked up in prison, and possibly executed.

As the soldiers and temple offers were still staggering under the power of God and regaining consciousness, the wound to Malchus' head was now gushing forth with blood. At that point, Luke the physician wrote, "And Jesus answered and said, suffer ye thus far. And he touched his ear, and healed him" (Luke 22:51). Notice the phrase "suffer ye this far." It is the equivalent of Jesus saying: *"Let Me just do one more thing before you take Me!"* Then He "touched" Malchus' ear and "healed" him.

The word "touched" is the Greek word *haptomai*, and it means *to firmly grasp or to hold tightly; to aggressively touch.* And the word "healed" is the Greek word *iaomai*, which means *to cure, to restore, or to heal.* Whether Jesus reached down and created a new ear for Malchus or He supernaturally knitted his severed ear back onto his head, we don't know. What we do know is that Jesus *aggressively grabbed* Malchus' head and held it firmly in His hands and restored his ear. Again, all this took place in the final hours just before Jesus was scourged and crucified on the Cross.

Who Was the Naked Boy in Gethsemane?

There is one more amazing miracle that took place the night Jesus was arrested in Gethsemane, and it is only recorded in Mark 14:51 and 52. It says, "And there followed him a certain young man, having a linen cloth cast about his naked body; and the young men laid hold on him: and he left the linen cloth, and fled from them naked."

The key to knowing the true identity of this young man is in understanding the original meaning of the words "linen cloth." It is the Greek word *sindon,* and it is used in the New Testament only to depict *a linen cloth in which individuals were wrapped for burial; thus, it is a burial shroud that was used for covering a dead body in the grave.* According to Jewish custom, when someone died, his body was ceremonially cleansed and placed in a grave or tomb with only a "linen cloth" covering his naked body.

As we noted at the opening of this lesson, Gethsemane had a sizable cemetery at its base. This means at any given time there were fresh graves with people that had just been buried. Apparently, when Jesus answered the soldiers with the words "I am" — *Ego eimi* — declaring He was God in the flesh, the lifeless corpse of a young man that had recently been buried in the Gethsemane cemetery was revived by the supernatural blast of power, and he was raised back to life.

Thus, the same power that caused the mob of soldiers and officers to stagger, stumble, and collapse to the ground as dead men also raised a dead man back to life! When the supernatural detonation of energy hit him, he came alive, crawled out of his grave, and stumbled onto the scene of Jesus' arrest with only his burial shroud to cover him.

When the armed men who were taking Jesus into custody saw this young man with only a burial shroud wrapped around him, they realized a resurrection had taken place. In an effort to squelch the news of another miraculous resurrection, they frantically reached out to grab hold of him, but he escaped their clutches, leaving behind his burial shroud in their hands.

Clearly, the end of Christ's ministry was just as miraculous as all that had taken place previously. Even as He was being arrested, He took the time to totally restore Malchus' ear and clean up Peter's mess. He released divine power through His words and knocked soldiers flat on their backs, and at the same time, raised a dead boy back to life. That same power is available to you right now! Jesus is the same yesterday, today, and forever! He was working miracles then, and He is still working miracles now. He stands ready and willing to change you and your situation — all you need to do is believe He will and invite Him in to do it!

STUDY QUESTIONS

Study to shew thyself approved unto God, a workman that needeth
not to be ashamed, rightly dividing the word of truth.
— 2 Timothy 2:15

1. What eye-opening facts did you learn from this lesson about the power of God on display in the Garden of Gethsemane the night Jesus was arrested?

2. When Jesus spoke, His words released power. Likewise, when you speak His Word, your words release power. Take time to meditate on Jeremiah 5:14; 23:28 and 29; and Hebrews 4:12. Ask the Holy Spirit to give you a revelation of the power of speaking God's Word. Also consider Proverbs 18:20, 21 and James 1:21.

PRACTICAL APPLICATION

But be ye doers of the word, and not hearers only,
deceiving your own selves.
— James 1:22

1. Peter's reckless actions were grounds for being arrested, tried, incarcerated, and possibly executed. But Jesus stepped in and miraculously cleaned up Peter's mess. What thoughtless mistakes have you made where God stepped in and spared you some serious consequences? How did it impact your future?

2. Just like the naked boy coming back to life in Gethsemane, people on the periphery of our lives are directly and indirectly resurrected by God's power at work in and through us. Stop and think, who in your life is suffering deathly symptoms and needs a resurrection? What do they need resurrected? Ask the Holy Spirit to reveal to you how to pray for them and what you can do to help them come back to life.

A Prayer To Receive Salvation

If you've never received Jesus as your Savior and Lord, now is the time for you to experience the new life Jesus wants to give you! To receive God's gift of salvation that can be obtained through Jesus alone, pray this prayer from your heart:

Jesus, I repent of my sin and receive You as my Savior and Lord. Wash away my sin with Your precious blood and make me completely new. I thank You that my sin is removed, and Satan no longer has any right to lay claim on me. Through Your empowering grace, I faithfully promise that I will serve You as my Lord for the rest of my life.

If you just prayed this prayer of salvation, you are born again! You are a brand-new creation in Christ! Would you please let us know of your decision by going to **renner.org/salvation**? We would love to connect with you and pray for you as you begin your new life in Christ.

Scriptures for further study: John 3:16; John 14:6; Acts 4:12; Ephesians 1:7; Hebrews 10:19,20; 1 Peter 1:18,19; Romans 10:9,10; Colossians 1:13; 2 Corinthians 5:17; Romans 6:4; 1 Peter 1:3

Notes

CLAIM YOUR FREE RESOURCE!

As a way of introducing you further to the teaching ministry of Rick Renner, we would like to send you FREE of charge his teaching, "How To Receive a Miraculous Touch From God" on CD or as an MP3 download.

How To Receive
a Miraculous Touch From God
Rick Renner
CD36
RENNER

In His earthly ministry, Jesus commonly healed *all* who were sick of *all* their diseases. In this profound message, learn about the manifold dimensions of Christ's wisdom, goodness, power, and love toward all humanity who came to Him in faith with their needs.

☑ **YES, I want to receive Rick Renner's monthly teaching letter!**

Simply scan the QR code to claim this resource or go to:
renner.org/claim-your-free-offer

Connect
WITH US!

renner.org

facebook.com/rickrenner • facebook.com/rennerdenise

youtube.com/rennerministries • youtube.com/deniserenner

instagram.com/rickrrenner • instagram.com/rennerministries_
instagram.com/rennerdenise